SECOND EDITION

TOUCHSTONE

STUDENT'S BOOK 2A

MICHAEL MCCARTHY

JEANNE MCCARTEN

HELEN SANDIFORD

CAMBRIDGE
UNIVERSITY PRESS

CAMBRIDGE
UNIVERSITY PRESS

32 Avenue of the Americas, New York, NY 10013-2473, USA

Cambridge University Press is part of the University of Cambridge.

It furthers the University's mission by disseminating knowledge in the pursuit of education, learning and research at the highest international levels of excellence.

www.cambridge.org
Information on this title: www.cambridge.org/9781107681750

First published 2005
Second Edition 2014
8th printing 2016

Printed in Italy by Rotolito Lombarda S.p.A.

A catalogue record for this publication is available from the British Library

ISBN 978-1-107-68173-6 Student's Book
ISBN 978-1-107-68175-0 Student's Book A
ISBN 978-1-107-62704-8 Student's Book B
ISBN 978-1-107-69037-0 Workbook
ISBN 978-1-107-64988-0 Workbook A
ISBN 978-1-107-61861-9 Workbook B
ISBN 978-1-107-65940-7 Full Contact
ISBN 978-1-107-61439-0 Full Contact A
ISBN 978-1-107-66547-7 Full Contact B
ISBN 978-1-107-62402-3 Teacher's Edition with Assessment Audio CD/CD-ROM
ISBN 978-1-107-67757-9 Class Audio CDs (4)

Additional resources for this publication at www.cambridge.org/touchstone2

Touchstone Second Edition has benefited from extensive development research. The authors and publishers would like to extend their thanks to the following reviewers and consultants for their valuable insights and suggestions:

Ana Lúcia da Costa Maia de Almeida and Mônica da Costa Monteiro de Souza from **IBEU**, Rio de Janeiro, Brazil; Andreza Cristiane Melo do Lago from **Magic English School**, Manaus, Brazil; Magaly Mendes Lemos from **ICBEU**, São José dos Campos, Brazil; Maria Lucia Zaorob, São Paulo, Brazil; Patricia McKay Aronis from **CEL LEP**, São Paulo, Brazil; Carlos Gontow, São Paulo, Brazil; Christiane Augusto Gomes da Silva from **Colégio Visconde de Porto Seguro**, São Paulo, Brazil; Silvana Fontana from **Lord's Idiomas**, São Paulo, Brazil; Alexander Fabiano Morishigue from **Speed Up Idiomas**, Jales, Brazil; Elisabeth Blom from **Casa Thomas Jefferson**, Brasília, Brazil; Michelle Dear from **International Academy of English**, Toronto, ON, Canada; Walter Duarte Marin, Laura Hurtado Portela, Jorge Quiroga, and Ricardo Suarez, from **Centro Colombo Americano**, Bogotá, Colombia; Jhon Jairo Castaneda Macias from **Praxis English Academy**, Bucaramanga, Colombia; Gloria Liliana Moreno Vizcaino from **Universidad Santo Tomas**, Bogotá, Colombia; Elizabeth Ortiz from **Copol English Institute (COPEI)**, Guayaquil, Ecuador; Henry Foster from **Kyoto Tachibana University**, Kyoto, Japan; Steven Kirk from **Tokyo University**, Tokyo, Japan; J. Lake from **Fukuoka Woman's University**, Fukuoka, Japan; Etsuko Yoshida from **Mie University**, Mie, Japan; B. Bricklin Zeff from **Hokkai Gakuen University**, Hokkaido, Japan; Ziad Abu-Hamatteh from **Al-Balqa' Applied University**, Al-Salt, Jordan; Roxana Pérez Flores from **Universidad Autonoma de Coahuila Language Center**, Saltillo, Mexico; Kim Alejandro Soriano Jimenez from **Universidad Politecnica de Altamira**, Altamira, Mexico; Tere Calderon Rosas from **Universidad Autonoma Metropolitana Campus Iztapalapa**, Mexico City, Mexico; Lilia Bondareva, Polina Ermakova, and Elena Frumina, from **National Research Technical University MISiS**, Moscow, Russia; Dianne C. Ellis from **Kyung Hee University**, Gyeonggi-do, South Korea; Jason M. Ham and Victoria Jo from **Institute of Foreign Language Education, Catholic University of Korea**, Gyeonggi-do, South Korea; Shaun Manning from **Hankuk University of Foreign Studies**, Seoul, South Korea; Natalie Renton from **Busan National University of Education**, Busan, South Korea; Chris Soutter from **Busan University of Foreign Studies**, Busan, South Korea; Andrew Cook from **Dong A University**, Busan, South Korea; Raymond Wowk from **Daejin University**, Gyeonggi-do, South Korea; Ming-Hui Hsieh and Jessie Huang from **National Central University**, Zhongli, Taiwan; Kim Phillips from **Chinese Culture University**, Taipei, Taiwan; Alex Shih from **China University of Technology**, Taipei Ta-Liao Township, Taiwan; Porntip Bodeepongse from **Thaksin University**, Songkhla, Thailand; Nattaya Puakpong and Pannathon Sangarun from **Suranaree University of Technology**, Nakhon Ratchasima, Thailand; Barbara Richards, Gloria Stewner-Manzanares, and Caroline Thompson, from **Montgomery College**, Rockville, MD, USA; Kerry Vrabel from **Gateway Community College**, Phoenix, AZ, USA.

Touchstone Second Edition authors and publishers would also like to thank the following individuals and institutions who have provided excellent feedback and support on *Touchstone Blended*:

Gordon Lewis, Vice President, Laureate Languages and Chris Johnson, Director, Laureate English Programs, Latin America from **Laureate International Universities**; **Universidad de las Americas**, Santiago, Chile; **University of Victoria**, Paris, France; **Universidad Technólogica Centroamericana**, Honduras; **Institut Universitaire de Casablanca**, Morocco; **Universidad Peruana de Ciencias Aplicadas**, Lima, Peru; **CIBERTEC**, Peru; **National Research Technical University (MiSIS)**, Moscow, Russia; **Institut Obert de Catalunya (IOC)**, Barcelona, Spain; Sedat Çilingir, Burcu Tezcan, and Didem Mutçalıoğlu from **İstanbul Bilgi Üniversitesi**, Istanbul, Turkey.

Touchstone Second Edition authors and publishers would also like to thank the following contributors to *Touchstone Second Edition*:

Sue Aldcorn, Frances Amrani, Deborah Gordon, Lisa Hutchins, Nancy Jordan, Steven Kirk, Genevieve Kocienda, Linda-Marie Koza, Geraldine Mark, Julianna Nielsen, Kathryn O'Dell, Nicola Prentis, Ellen Shaw, Kristin Sherman, Luis Silva Susa, Mary Vaughn, Kerry S. Vrabel, Shari Young, and Eric Zuarino.

Authors' Acknowledgments

The authors would like to thank all the Cambridge University Press staff and freelancers who were involved in the creation of *Touchstone Second Edition*. In addition, they would like to acknowledge a huge debt of gratitude that they owe to two people: Mary Vaughn, for her role in creating *Touchstone First Edition* and for being a constant source of wisdom ever since, and Bryan Fletcher, who also had the vision that has led to the success of *Touchstone Blended Learning*.

Helen Sandiford would like to thank her family for their love and support, especially her husband Bryan.

The author team would also like to thank each other, for the joy of working together, sharing the same professional dedication, and for the mutual support and friendship.

Finally, the authors would like to thank our dear friend Alejandro Martinez, Global Training Manager, who sadly passed away in 2012. He is greatly missed by all who had the pleasure to work with him. Alex was a huge supporter of *Touchstone* and everyone is deeply grateful to him for his contribution to its success.

Touchstone Level 2A Contents and learning outcomes

	Learning outcomes	Language		
		Grammar	Vocabulary	Pronunciation
Unit 1 **Making friends** pages 1–10	• Ask questions to get to know your classmates using the simple present • Talk about your favorite things • Use responses with *too* and *either* to show what you have in common • Start conversations with people you don't know • Use *actually* to give new or surprising information • Read an article about small talk • Write a *How-to* article using correct punctuation	• Review of simple present and present of *be* in questions and statements • Responses with *too* and *either* ***Extra practice***	• Review of types of TV shows, clothes, food, and weekend activities	***Speaking naturally*** • Stress and intonation in questions and answers ***Sounds right*** • Hard and soft consonants
Unit 2 **Interests** pages 11–20	• Talk about your interests with *can, like, hate, prefer, be good at*, etc. • Discuss your taste in music using object pronouns and *everyone, nobody*, etc. • Say *no* in a friendly way • Use *really / not really* to make statements stronger / softer • Read an online forum about hobbies • Write online forum posts using linking expressions	• Verb forms after *can / can't, love, like*, etc., and prepositions • Object pronouns • *Everybody, everyone, nobody*, and *no one* ***Extra practice***	• Interests and hobbies • Types of music	***Speaking naturally*** • Saying lists ***Sounds right*** • Matching vowel sounds
Unit 3 **Health** pages 21–30	• Talk about exercise and how to stay healthy using the simple present and present continuous • Discuss common health problems using *if* and *when* • Encourage people to say more • Use expressions like *Really?* and *Oh!* to show surprise • Read an article about staying healthy • Write questions and answers about health concerns	• Simple present and present continuous • Joining clauses with *if* and *when* ***Extra practice***	• Ways to stay healthy • Common health problems • Common remedies	***Speaking naturally*** • Contrasts ***Sounds right*** • Matching vowel sounds
Checkpoint Units 1–3 pages 31–32				
Unit 4 **Celebrations** pages 33–42	• Talk about gift giving and birthdays using *be going to* and indirect objects • Talk about how you celebrate special days • Talk about plans using the present continuous or *be going to* • Use "vague" expressions like *and everything* • Give vague responses like *It depends* if you're not sure • Read an article about traditions around the world • Write an invitation to a special event	• Future with *be going to* • Indirect objects • Indirect object pronouns • Present continuous for the future ***Extra practice***	• Months of the year • Days of the month • Special days, celebrations, and holidays • Things people do to celebrate special days	***Speaking naturally*** • Reduction of *going to* ***Sounds right*** • Which sound in each group is different?
Unit 5 **Growing up** pages 43–52	• Talk about growing up and your family background using the simple past • Talk about school subjects people studied using *most (of), a few (of)*, etc. • Correct things you say with expressions like *Well, Actually*, and *No, wait* • Use *I mean* to correct a word or name • Read an interview about a man's teenage years • Write answers to interview questions	• *be born* • Review of simple past in questions and statements • General and specific use of determiners ***Extra practice***	• Time expressions for the past • Saying years • School subjects	***Speaking naturally*** • Reduction of *did you* ***Sounds right*** • Hard and soft consonant sounds
Unit 6 **Around town** pages 53–62	• Ask about places with *Is there . . . ?* and *Are there . . . ?* • Say where places are with *next to, between*, etc. • Ask for and give directions • Offer and ask for help with *Can* and *Could* • Check information by repeating words or using expressions like *Excuse me?* • Ask "echo" questions like *It's where?* to check • Read an online guide to Istanbul • Write a walking-tour guide	• *Is there?* and *Are there?* • Pronouns *one* and *ones* • Offers and requests with *Can* and *Could* ***Extra practice***	• Places in town • Location expressions • Expressions for asking and giving directions	***Speaking naturally*** • Word stress in compound nouns ***Sounds right*** • Matching vowel sounds spelled with *a* and *o*
Checkpoint Units 4–6 pages 63–64				

Interaction	Skills				Self study
Conversation strategies	Listening	Reading	Writing	Free talk	Vocabulary notebook
• Start a conversation with someone you don't know • Use *actually* to give or to "correct" information	**What's the question?** • Listen to answers and match them with questions **This is a great party!** • Listen to responses and match them to conversation starters; then listen for more information	**Improve your skills and "small talk" your way to success** • A magazine article giving advice	**How to improve . . .** • Write an article giving advice on how to improve something • Review of punctuation	**Sally's party!** • Group work: Play a game to make small talk at a party	**Webs of words** • Use word webs to organize new vocabulary
• Say *no* in a friendly way • Use *really* and *not really* to make statements stronger or softer	**Interesting hobbies** • Match conversations about hobbies with photos; fill in a chart **Favorite websites** • Listen for details as two people talk about a website	• Read an online forum	**A message board** • Write a question to post on a message board • Link ideas with *and*, *also*, *especially*, *or*, *but*, and *because*	**Common interests** • Group work: Ask and answer questions about your own hobbies	**I really like to sing!** • Link new words together in word "chains"
• Encourage people to say more to keep a conversation going • Show surprise	**Unhealthy habits** • Predict what people will say about their habits; listen to check **Coping with stress** • Match conversations about relaxing with photos; listen for details	**Rethink your way to great health** • Read an article about improving personal health	**That's great advice!** • Write a question asking advice about a health problem, and write replies to your classmates' questions • Use commas after *if* and *when* clauses	**True or false?** • Pair work: Ask questions to guess true and untrue information about habits	**Under the weather** • Write down words you can use with a new word or expression

Checkpoint Units 1–3 pages 31–32

• Use "vague" expressions like *and everything* • Give "vague" responses like *I don't know* and *Maybe* when you're not sure	**Celebrations around the world** • Listen to people talk about two festivals, and answer questions **Congratulations!** • Listen for details in two conversations about invitations, and fill in the blanks	**Let's celebrate!** • Read an article about traditions in different countries	**Congratulations!** • Write an invitation to a special event, and add a personal note • Formal and informal ways to begin and end a note or letter	**A new celebration** • Group work: Create a new special day or festival, and talk about it with other groups	**Calendars** • Write new vocabulary about special days and celebrations on a calendar
• Correct things you say with expressions like *Well, Actually,* and *No, wait* • Use *I mean* to correct yourself when you say the wrong word or name	**I don't remember exactly . . .** • Listen for corrections as people talk about childhood memories **A long time ago** • Listen for details as a man talks about his teenage years	**Teenage years** • Read an interview with a man who talks about his teenage years	**An interview** • Write interview questions to ask a classmate about when he or she was younger, and reply to a classmate's questions • Link ideas with *except (for)* and *apart from*	**In the past** • Class activity: Ask your classmates questions about their childhood, and take notes	**I hated math!** • Group new vocabulary in different ways
• Repeat key words to check information • Use "checking" expressions to check information • Use "echo" questions to check information	**Finding your way around** • Match four sets of directions with the destinations by following the map **Tourist information** • Listen to conversations at a visitor center, and predict what each person says next to check the information	**3 days in Istanbul . . .** • Read a travel website about Istanbul	**A walking-tour guide** • Write a guide for a walking tour of your city or town • Expressions for giving directions	**Apartment hunting** • Pair work: Ask and answer questions about two apartments, and choose one to live in	**Which way?** • Draw and label a map to remember directions

Checkpoint Units 4–6 pages 63–64

Useful language for . . .

Getting help

How do you say "_____" in English?

I'm sorry. What did you say?

How do you say this word?

What do we have to do?

I don't understand. What do you mean?

Do you mean _____?

Can you spell "_____" for me, please?

Working with a partner

Whose turn is it now?

It's my / your turn.

Do you want to go first?

OK. I'll go first. / No, you go first.

This time we change roles.

OK. I'll start.

Are we done?

Yes, I think so. Let's try it again.

Let's compare answers.

OK. What do you have for number 1?

Do you have _____ for number 3?

No, I have _____. Let's check again.

Do you understand this sentence?

Yeah. It means "_____."

Making friends

 Can Do! In this unit, you learn how to . . .

Lesson A	Lesson B	Lesson C	Lesson D
• Ask questions to get to know your classmates using the simple present	• Talk about your favorite things • Use responses with *too* and *either* to show what you have in common	• Start conversations with people you don't know • Use *actually* to give new or surprising information	• Read an article about small talk • Write a *How-to* article using correct punctuation

Before you begin . . .

Where do people make friends? What questions can you ask a new friend about these topics?

- school or work
- home and family
- free time
- favorite things

How well do you know your new CLASSMATES?

YOUR NAME

1. What's your name? _____
2. What does your name mean? _____
_____
3. Are you named after someone? _____
4. Do you like your name? _____
5. *Do you have a middle name?* _____
_____

LIFESTYLE

1. Are you a full-time student? _____
   a. If *yes*: What's your major? _____
   b. If *no*: What do you do for a living? _____
2. How do you get to work (or class)? _____
3. How long does it take? _____
4. _____
_____

HOME AND FAMILY

1. Where do you live? _____
2. Do you like your neighborhood? _____
3. Do you live alone or with your family? _____
4. Where are your parents from? _____
5. _____
_____

FRIENDS

1. Do you often make friends online? _____
2. What's your best friend like? _____
3. What does your best friend do? _____
4. What do you and your friends do when you get together? _____
5. _____
_____

1 Getting started

About you **Pair work** Write one more question in each section of the questionnaire. Then interview a partner and take notes.

B **Pair work** Tell a new partner five interesting things about your first partner.

2 Speaking naturally Stress and intonation

> *Do you have a nickname?*   *Are you from a big family?*   *What do you do for fun?*
>
> *Yes. People call me Jimmy.*   *Yes. I have four sisters.*   *I go to the movies.*

A 🔊 1.02 Listen and repeat the questions and answers above. Notice the stress on the important content word. Notice how the voice rises, or rises and then falls, on the stressed word.

About you **Pair work** Ask and answer the questions. Give your own answers.

③ Grammar Present of *be* and simple present (review) ◀)) 1.03

Extra practice p. 140

Present of *be*

Are you from a big family?
 Yes, I **am**. I'm one of six children.
 No, I'm **not**. There **are** only two of us.

Are you and your friends full-time students?
 Yes, we **are**. We're English majors.
 No, we're **not**. We're part-time students.

What's your name? **Is** it Leo?
 Yes, it **is**. My name's Leo Green.
 No, it's **not**. My name **isn't** Leo. It's Joe.

Where **are** your parents from? **Are** they from Peru?
 Yes, they **are**. They're from Lima.
 No, they're **not**. My parents **aren't** from Peru.

Simple present

Do you **have** any brothers and sisters?
 Yes, I **do**. I **have** a brother.
 No, I **don't**. I'm an only child.

Do you and your friends **get together** a lot?
 Yes, we **do**. We **go out** all the time.
 No, we **don't**. We **don't have** time.

What **does** your brother **do**? **Does** he **go** to college?
 Yes, he **does**. He **goes** to the same college as me.
 No, he **doesn't**. He **works** at a bank.

Where **do** your parents **live**? **Do** they **live** nearby?
 Yes, they **do**. They **live** near here.
 No, they **don't**. They **don't live** around here.

A Think of a possible question for each answer. Compare with a partner.

1. A _Are you an only brother_ ?
   B No, I'm not. I have a brother and a sister.

2. A _What does your sister do_ ?
   B She works at a software company.

3. A _Do you have a car_ ?
   B No, I don't. I usually use my dad's car.

4. A _what color do you like_ ?
   B Turquoise. And I like blue, too.

5. A _Are your parents from here_ ?
   B Yeah, they are. My grandparents are from here, too.

6. A _what do you and your friends do on weekends_ ?
   B We usually go shopping or have lunch.

7. A _Does your sister live with you_ ?
   B No, she doesn't. She lives an hour away.

8. A _what are your classmates like?_ ?
   B My classmates? They're all smart.

Pair work Ask your questions. Give your own answers.

④ Listening and speaking What's the question?

A ◀)) 1.04 Listen to Miranda's answers to these questions. Number the questions 1 to 6.

☐ Do you have any pets?
☐ Do you ever go out on weeknights?
☐ What's your favorite band?

☐1 What's your favorite season?
☐ How much time do you spend with your family?
☐ What do you usually do on the weekends?

B ◀)) 1.04 Listen again. What do you learn about Miranda? Take notes for each question.

About you **Pair work** Ask and answer the questions above. Ask your partner follow-up questions to keep the conversations going.

❌ Common errors

Use *do* or *does* in simple present questions.

*What **do** you study?*
*Where **does** your family live?*
(NOT ~~*What you study?*~~
~~*Where your family live?*~~)

1 Building language

A 🔊 1.05 Listen. What do these friends have in common? Practice the conversations.

❶
A Dogs are so noisy, and they always wreck things. I'm just not an animal lover, I guess.
B Well, I'm not either. I'm allergic to dogs and cats.

❷
A I don't watch much television.
B No, I don't either.
A I mean, I watch pro football.
B Yeah, I do too. But that's about it.

❸
A I love shopping. I can shop for hours! Too bad I can't afford anything new.
B I know. I can't either. I'm broke.
A Yeah, I am too.

Figure it out **B** Complete the responses so the speakers agree. Use the conversations above to help you.

1. A I'm a football fan.
   B Yes, I am _do too_.

2. A I love shopping.
   B Oh, I do _too_.

3. A I don't like animals.
   B No, I don't _either_.

4. A I can't have a pet.
   B I can't _either_.

2 Grammar   Responses with *too* and *either* 🔊 1.06

Extra practice p. 140

Present of *be*	Simple present	*can*
I**'m** allergic to cats.	I **watch** pro football.	I **can** shop for hours!
I **am too**.	I **do too**.	I **can too**.
I**'m not** an animal lover.	I **don't watch** much television.	I **can't** afford anything new.
I**'m not either**.	I **don't either**.	I **can't either**.

People also respond with *Me too* and *Me neither* (or *Me either*).

In conversation

People actually say *Me either* more often than *Me neither*.

▬▬▬ *Me either.*

▬ *Me neither.*

A Respond to these statements using *too* or *either*. Then practice with a partner.

1. I watch a lot of sports on TV. *I do too.*
2. I'm allergic to nuts.
3. I can't afford a new laptop.
4. I'm not a morning person.
5. I don't have a pet.
6. I can eat chocolate all day.

About you **Pair work** Student A: Make the statements above true for you.
Student B: Give your own responses.

A I don't watch a lot of sports on TV.

B I don't either.   **OR**   *Really? I watch all the basketball games.*

❸ Building vocabulary

A Brainstorm! How many other words can you think of for each topic? Make a class list.

WEEKEND ACTIVITIES	TV SHOWS	FOOD	CLOTHES

play sports eat out sleep late go to a club	the news talk shows cartoons documentaries	fruit fish vegetables ice cream	a sweater a dress a suit a jacket

Word sort

Pair work Complete the chart with your favorite things. Compare with a partner.
Then tell the class what you and your partner have in common.

weekend activities	TV shows	food	clothes
eat out Sleep late go to a movie run in the park read novels	The news movies	fruit vegetables	a dress a sweater a jeans

A *I eat out on the weekends.*
B *I do too.*

⎤ *"We both eat out on the weekends."*

📓 **Vocabulary notebook** p. 10

About you

Class activity Complete the sentences with your likes and dislikes.
Then tell your classmates your sentences. Find someone with the same tastes.

My tastes	Classmate with same taste
1. I love _____ Como titai_____ . (type of food)	_____
2. I don't _____run____ very often. (weekend activity)	_____
3. I like to wear ____dress____ . (item of clothing)	_____
4. I'm not a big _baseball_ fan. (sport)	_____
5. I like ____black____ . (color)	_____
6. I can't stand _Talk shows_ . (type or name of TV show)	_____
7. I hate _pork and seafood_ . (type of food)	_____

A *I love pineapple.*
B *I do too.*   **OR**   *Oh really? I don't like it so much.*

It's cold tonight.

1 Conversation strategy Starting a conversation

A What are good topics to talk about when you meet someone for the first time?
Check (✓) the boxes.

☐ your salary   ☑ your family   ☑ the weather   ☐ someone's appearance
☐ your health   ☑ where you live   ☐ your problems   ☐ things you see around you

B 🔊 1.07 Listen. What topics do Eve and Chris talk about?

Eve	Ooh, it's cold tonight.
Chris	Yeah, it is. But actually, I kind of like cold weather.
Eve	You do? Really? . . . Boy, there are a lot of people out here tonight.
Chris	Yeah, it gets pretty crowded on weekends.
Eve	Do you come here a lot?
Chris	Yeah, I do, actually.
Eve	So are you a big hip-hop fan?
Chris	Yeah, I am. Are you?
Eve	Actually, no, but my brother's in the band tonight.
Chris	Oh, really? Cool. . . . By the way, my name's Chris.
Eve	Nice to meet you. I'm Eve.

C Notice how Eve starts a conversation with a stranger.
She talks about the things around them, like the
weather and the club, and asks general questions.
Find examples in the conversation.

Ooh, it's cold tonight.
Do you come here a lot?

D Pair work Think of a situation where you could use each conversation starter below.
Compare with a partner. Then role-play the conversations.

1. "The flowers are beautiful, huh? I love spring."   *on a bench in a park*
2. "Gosh, it's so crowded here. And it's hot!"   _____
3. "Wow. The elevator is really slow today."   _____
4. "Hi there. It's windy, huh?"   _____
5. "Hmm. This food doesn't look too good."   _____
6. "I'm a bit nervous. Is it your first class, too?"   _____

2 Strategy plus *Actually*

You can use *actually* to give new or surprising information.

But actually, I kind of like cold weather.

You can also use *actually* to "correct" things people say or think.

A So, you're American?
B Well, actually, I'm from Canada.

> **In conversation**
>
> *Actually* is one of the top 200 words.

A Match each conversation starter with a response. Then practice with a partner.

1. It's really chilly in here. _b_
2. Is this your first class here? ____
3. So, you're a full-time student? ____
4. Do you like this neighborhood? ____
5. Do you drive to class? ____
6. I like your sweater. ____
7. Do you play guitar or anything? ____
8. So, you're from around here? ____

a. Actually, I take the subway. It takes an hour.
b. It's the air conditioning. Actually, I feel OK.
c. Yes, it is, actually. I'm a little nervous.
d. Thanks. It's actually from a vintage store.
e. No, actually I'm from a small town about three hours away.
f. Yeah, I do, actually. It has some great stores.
g. Um, part-time, actually. I work in a hotel.
h. Actually, I do. And piano.

About you

Pair work Start conversations using the ideas above. Use *actually* in your responses if you need to.

"It's pretty warm in here."   *"Yeah it is, but I kind of like it, actually."*

3 Listening and strategies This is a great party!

A 🔊 1.08 Listen to six people talk at Tom's party. Which conversation starters are the people responding to? Number the sentences 1 to 6.

☐ Great music, huh?
☐ Are you a friend of Tom's?
[1] This is a great party.
☐ The desserts look good.
☐ Is it me, or is it really hot in here?
☐ I don't really know anyone here. Do you?

B 🔊 1.09 Now listen to the complete conversations. Check your answers. What six things do you find out about Tom?

About you

Class activity Imagine you are at a class party. Start conversations with your classmates. Find out something new about six classmates.

A *I like your jacket.*
B *Thanks. Actually, it's from a vintage store.*

Free talk p. 129

7

1 Reading

A What is small talk? When do people use small talk? Tell the class.

B Read the title of the article and the introduction on the left. Think of a tip. Then read the whole article. Was your tip mentioned?

> **Reading tip**
>
> First, read and think about the title. Try to predict three ideas in the article.

Improve
your skills and
"SMALL TALK"
your way to
success

According to some surveys, the ability to make small talk is important for social and professional success. Chatting about topics like the weather or weekends helps you connect with people, and that can be the key to making friends or business contacts. You don't have to be outgoing to make small talk. Just follow these easy tips.

1 **S**MILE and say "Hello" when you meet someone new. Say your name and shake hands. Try to repeat the person's name: "Nice to meet you, Mariana."

2 **M**AKE a comment about your surroundings – for example, the weather ("It's really cold today.") or the event ("There are a lot of people here.").

3 **A**SK questions. Try to find something you have in common: "Are you new to the company, too?" However, don't ask very personal questions, for example about someone's salary or age.

4 **L**ISTEN actively. Show interest with comments like "Oh, really?" or "That's interesting." Keep eye contact, and don't look around the room during your conversation.

5 **L**EARN about what's going on in the world, so you can add to any discussion.

6 **T**AKE your time. Don't rush the conversation, and don't look at your watch. It can seem rude.

7 **A**NSWER people's questions with interesting or funny stories. People love stories and will remember you.

8 **L**EAVE politely. To end a conversation, say something like, "Well, it was nice talking to you." or "Great meeting you. Good luck with your job search!"

9 **K**EEP in touch. Send a quick email or text message. Say, "It was good to meet you."

C Read the sentences below. Which tips from the article are they examples of? Write the number of the tip.

1. "Well, it was great talking with you. By the way, here's my card." _____
2. "So, what kind of work do you do?" _____
3. "The desserts look really good." _____
4. "Hi, Carlos. Pleased to meet you. I'm Frank." _____
5. "Wow! That sounds amazing!" _____
6. "Well, I often go biking on the weekends. Actually, last weekend I got lost and . . ." _____

D Pair work Discuss the questions below.

1. Read tip 2 again. Can you think of another example comment?

2. Read tip 3 again. What other good questions can you think of?

3. Read tip 5 again. What is going on in the world at the moment? Choose two topics that you can use in a conversation.

4. Read tip 7 again. Do you have a funny story you can tell? What is it?

5. Can you think of one more tip on how to improve your "small talk" skills?

2 Writing How to improve . . .

A Brainstorm ideas for each topic and write notes.

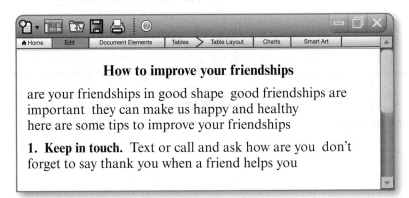

Improve your friendships
1. offer to do a favor for a friend
2. give compliments

Improve your social life

Improve your English

B Read the Help note and the extract from an article below. Correct the punctuation.

| ♠ Home | Edit | Document Elements | Tables | Table Layout | Charts | Smart Art |

How to improve your friendships

are your friendships in good shape good friendships are important they can make us happy and healthy here are some tips to improve your friendships

1. Keep in touch. Text or call and ask how are you don't forget to say thank you when a friend helps you

Help note

Punctuation
- Use a CAPITAL letter to start a sentence.
- Use a comma (,) before quotation marks (" ") and in lists.
- Use a period (.) at the end of a statement and a question mark (?) at the end of a question.

C Write an article on one of the topics you brainstormed above. Give three tips. Then read a partner's article and check the punctuation. Can you think of another tip?

3 Talk about it Friendly conversations

Group work Discuss the questions. Find out about your classmates' conversation styles.

▸ When do you make small talk? What do you talk about?

▸ Do you think it's odd when a stranger talks to you?

▸ Are you a talkative person?

▸ Do you think you talk too much?

▸ Are you a good listener?

▸ Are you usually the "talker" or the "listener" in a conversation?

▸ What topics do you like to talk about?

▸ What topics do you try to avoid?

(((Sounds right p. 137

9

Learning tip *Word webs*

You can use word webs to organize your new vocabulary.

1 Complete the word webs for *clothes* and *food* using words from the box.

bread ✓jacket   jeans   pineapple   rice   skirt   sweatshirt   yogurt

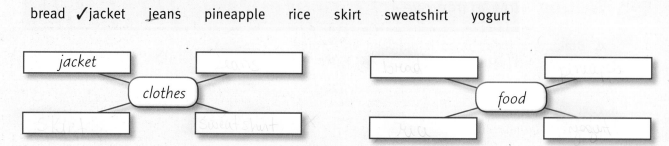

jacket	
	clothes
skirt	sweatshirt

bread	
	food
rice	yogurt

2 Now make word webs about *colors* and *TV shows*. Write a sentence about each word.

I never wear purple.

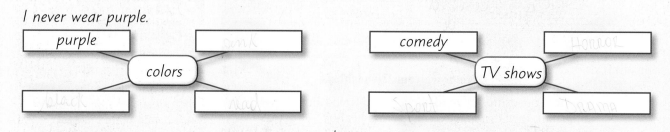

purple	pink
	colors
black	red

comedy	Horror
	TV shows
sport	Drama

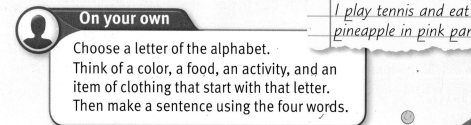

On your own

Choose a letter of the alphabet.
Think of a color, a food, an activity, and an item of clothing that start with that letter.
Then make a sentence using the four words.

I play tennis and eat pineapple in pink pants.

Can Do! Now I can . . .

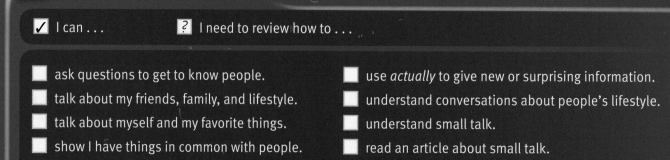

✓ I can . . .   ? I need to review how to . . .

- [ ] ask questions to get to know people.
- [ ] talk about my friends, family, and lifestyle.
- [ ] talk about myself and my favorite things.
- [ ] show I have things in common with people.
- [ ] start conversations with people I don't know.

- [ ] use *actually* to give new or surprising information.
- [ ] understand conversations about people's lifestyle.
- [ ] understand small talk.
- [ ] read an article about small talk.
- [ ] write a *How-to* article.

Interests

 Can Do! In this unit, you learn how to . . .

Lesson A
- Talk about your interests with *can*, *like*, *hate*, *prefer*, *be good at*, etc.

Lesson B
- Discuss your taste in music, using object pronouns and *everyone*, *nobody*, etc.

Lesson C
- Say *no* in a friendly way
- Use *really* and *not really* to make statements stronger or softer

Lesson D
- Read an online forum about hobbies
- Write posts for an online forum using linking expressions

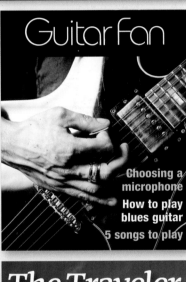

Guitar Fan

Choosing a microphone

How to play blues guitar

5 songs to play

Health and Fitness

Your guide to running

Foods for energy

Daily stretches

Better Gardens

BIGGER, BETTER TOMATOES

GET MORE FROM SMALL SPACES

20 RECIPES FOR FRESH VEGETABLES

The Traveler

Traveling on a budget

10 GREAT PLACES FOR YOUR NEXT VACATION

Affordable trips for college students

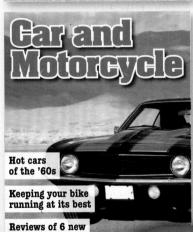

Car and Motorcycle

Hot cars of the '60s

Keeping your bike running at its best

Reviews of 6 new sport bikes

FASHION ZONE

New looks for men

Fabulous accessories every woman wants

Spring fashion guide

Before you begin . . .
Look at the magazine covers. Which magazines would you like to read? Why?

College News

Meet our new reporter for the *College News*...

The *College News* interviewed Brad Hayes, our new reporter. Brad is a full-time student majoring in journalism. We asked him about his hobbies.

❶ College News: *What are your hobbies?*

Brad Hayes: Well, I enjoy writing. I like to do a bit of creative writing every day – in the evenings mostly. Someday I want to write a novel, but for now it's just a hobby.

❷ CN: _____

Brad: Let's see, what else? Well, I design cards. I'm good at drawing, and I'm really into computer graphics, so I sit and learn new programs, and I play around with them.

❸ CN: _____

Brad: Yeah, I play the saxophone, and I can play the piano a little, but not very well. I'd like to play in a jazz band or something. And I like to sing, but I really can't sing at all.

❹ CN: _____

Brad: Not really. I prefer to watch sports on TV. I like to play pool. Is that a sport? I guess I jog occasionally. But I hate going to the gym and working out.

❺ CN: _____

Brad: Yeah. I love to do new stuff all the time – learn new skills, you know. I'm really excited about writing for the *College News*.

1 Getting started

A What kinds of things do students do in their leisure time? Make a list.

B 🔊 1.10 Listen to student reporter Brad answer these five questions. Number the questions 1 to 5. Then write them in the interview.

☐ Are you good at sports?
☐ Can you play a musical instrument?
☐ Are you interested in learning new things?

[1] What are your hobbies?
☐ What else do you enjoy doing in your free time?

C 🔊 1.11 Listen to the complete interview. Underline the things Brad likes to do. Circle the things he hates doing.

Figure it out

Circle the correct forms of the verbs to complete the sentences. Which sentences are true for you? Tell a partner.

1. I can **play** / **to play** the piano.
2. I like **to watch** / **watch** sports on TV.
3. I enjoy **listening** / **to listen** to music.
4. I'm good at **learn** / **learning** new skills.

2 Grammar Verb forms 🔊 1.12

Extra practice p. 141

can / can't + verb	Verb + to + verb	Verb + verb + -ing	Preposition + verb + -ing
I can **play** the piano.	I love **to swim**.	I love **swimming**.	I'm good at **drawing** people.
I can't **play** very well.	I like **to play** pool.	I like **playing** pool.	I'm not interested in **skiing**.
I can't **sing** at all.	I hate **to work out**.	I hate **working out**.	
	I prefer **to watch** TV.	I prefer **watching** TV.	
	I'd like **to play** jazz.	I enjoy **reading**.	

A Complete the conversations. Sometimes more than one answer is possible. Then practice with a partner.

1. A Do you enjoy ___cooking___ (cook)?
   B Actually, yeah. I like ___to make___ (make) my own bread, too.

2. A Are you good at ___reading___ (read) music?
   B No, but I can ___play___ (play) music by ear.

3. A What kinds of games do you enjoy ___playing___ (play)? Do you like to ___play___ (play) games online?
   B No. I hate ___to sit___ (sit) at the computer in my free time.

4. A Are you interested in ___joining___ (join) a gym class?
   B Well, I enjoy ___going___ (go) to the gym, but I'm not interested in ___taking___ (take) a class. I'd like ___to start___ (start) tennis lessons though.

5. A How do you like ___to spend___ (spend) an evening? Do you prefer _____ (be) alone or with friends?
   B That's easy. I love ___to eat out___ (eat out) with my friends.

In conversation

I like / love / hate to + verb
is more common than
I like / love / hate + verb + *-ing.*

▮▮▮▮▮▮ *I like to . . .*
▮ *I like . . . ing*
▮▮▮▮ *I love to . . .*
▮ *I love . . . ing*
▮▮▮▮ *I hate to . . .*
▮ *I hate . . . ing*

✗ Common errors

Remember: *I'd like = I want.*

I'd like to find a piano teacher.
(NOT I ~~like~~ to find . . .)

Pair work Ask and answer the questions above and in Brad's interview. Give your own answers.

3 Survey What are your interests?

Class activity Write questions in the chart. Then ask your classmates the questions and take notes.

Find someone who . . .	Question	Name	Notes
1. can sing really well	*Can you sing really well?*	*Pablo*	*He can whistle, too!*
2. likes to read or write blogs			
3. hates dancing			
4. can ride a motorcycle			
5. is good at playing guitar			
6. enjoys horseback riding			

B Tell the class about someone on your list.

"Pablo sings really well. He sings pop songs, and he can whistle, too."

1 Building vocabulary

A 🔊 **1.13** Listen. Number the types of music you hear. What other kinds of music do you know?

☐ rock music   ☐ hip-hop and rap   ☐ pop music   ☐ classical music

☐ country music   ☐ folk music   ☐ jazz   ☐ Latin music

Word sort Complete the chart with the words above. Add ideas. Then compare with a partner.

I love . . .	I like . . .	I don't care for . . .	I can't stand . . .
pop music	Classical music	electronic music	folk music
latin music	rock music	Country music	hip-hop and rap
		rock music	

A *I love pop music.*
B *Yeah, I do too. Adele is my favorite singer.*

Vocabulary notebook p. 20

2 Speaking naturally Saying lists

Jim What kinds of music do you like?

*Sam I like **classical**, and **hip-hop**, and **jazz**.*   *Silvia I like **pop**, and **rock**, and **folk**, . . .*

A 🔊 **1.14** Listen and repeat the sentences above. Notice that Sam's list is complete, but Silvia's list is not.

About you **Class activity** Ask your classmates, *What kinds of music do you like?* What are the most popular answers?

3 Building language

A 🔊 **1.15** **Listen. What does Carla think of the band? Practice the conversation.**

Alex   Listen. What do you think of this song?

Carla   It's good – I like it. Who is it?

Alex   A new band . . . some local guys. Do you like them?

Carla   They're local? Really? They're pretty good. Who's the lead
        singer? I like her. She sounds like Mariah Carey.

Alex   Yeah, everybody says that. It's my friend Lori.

Carla   Who's the guy singing with her? I'm not sure about him.

Alex   Uh . . . actually, that's me. I'm in the band, too.

Figure
it out

**Complete the questions with your own ideas. Circle the correct words
in the answers. Then ask and answer your questions with a partner.**

1. A What do you think of _____ (male singer)?   B I like **him / it / them**.

2. A Do you know _____ (female singer)?   B Yeah, I love **him / her / them**.

3. A Do you like _____ (band)?   B Yeah, Everybody **like / likes** their music.

4 Grammar   Object pronouns; *everybody, nobody* 🔊 **1.16**

Extra practice p. 141

Object pronouns
I'm a singer. That's **me** on the CD.
You're a musician? I'd like to hear **you**.
She's pretty good. I like **her**.
He's not local. I don't know **him**.

It's a nice song. I like **it**.
We play in a band. Come listen to **us**.
They're local guys. Do you like **them**?

Everybody, nobody
Everybody say**s** that.
Everyone like**s** pop.
Nobody is a jazz fan.
No one listen**s** to rap.

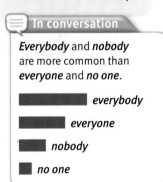

💬 **In conversation**

Everybody and *nobody*
are more common than
everyone and *no one*.

▬▬▬▬▬ *everybody*
▬▬▬ *everyone*
▬▬ *nobody*
▬ *no one*

**A Complete the conversations. Use object pronouns or the correct form
    of the verbs given. Then practice with a partner.**

1. A I love classical music. Everyone in my family ___*likes*___ (like) ___*it*___ .

    B Really? Nobody in my house _____ (listen) to classical music.

2. A I like to watch talent shows. Do you like _____ ?

    B I do, actually. Do you know Javier Colon? He was a winner.
       I like _____ .

    A Yeah. It's amazing. Nobody _____ (know) these people,
       and then the next day everybody _____ (love) _____ .

3. A Do you know Taylor Swift? She's great. I like _____ .

    B Oh yeah. My friend and I saw _____ in concert. She smiled at _____ !

4. A My favorite band is Coldplay. They're great in concert. Do you like _____ ?

    B Yeah. No one _____ (write) music like they do. And Chris Martin – he's got
       a great voice. Too bad I can't sing like _____ !

About
you

Pair work Practice the conversations above with your own ideas.

A *I love The Beatles. We listen to them a lot.*

B *Yeah. I think everyone likes them.*

1 Conversation strategy Saying *no* in a friendly way

A How many hobbies and interests can you think of in 30 seconds? Make a list.

B 🔊 1.17 Listen. What hobbies do Sarah and Greg have?

Sarah	Hmm, that smells really good. What is it?
Greg	Homemade lasagna.
Sarah	Nice. Do you do a lot of cooking?
Greg	Not really. But I like to make pasta dishes. How about you? Do you enjoy cooking?
Sarah	Um, no, not really. I mean, I cook every day, but I'm not really into it.
Greg	So what do you do in your free time? Do you have any hobbies, or . . . ?
Sarah	Well no, I don't really have much time. But I do a little photography. I have a blog and post my photos on it.
Greg	Yeah? I'd really like to take a look sometime.
Sarah	Sure. I can email you the link. Or stop by my desk later, and I can show you some photos.

C **Notice** how Sarah and Greg say more than just *no* when they answer questions. They want to be friendly or polite. Find examples in the conversation.

> *Um, no, not really. I mean,*
> *I cook every day, but . . .*

D Match the questions and answers. Then practice with a partner.

1. Are you into photography? _d_
2. Do you read a lot? ____
3. Are you good at fixing things? ____
4. Are you interested in sports? ____
5. Do you do any martial arts? ____
6. Do you like to play board games? ____
7. Can you swim? I mean, are you a good swimmer? ____

a. No, I'm not really good with my hands. Are you?
b. No, not really. But I like to go to the pool.
c. No, not really. I enjoy doing puzzles, though. Like Sudoku.
d. Not really. I mean, I take pictures. But I never edit them or anything.
e. No. I don't have a lot of free time. I look at magazines sometimes.
f. Not really. But I like to watch the Olympics.
g. No, but my sister does. She does Tae Kwon Do.

About you **Pair work** Ask and answer the questions. Give your own answers.

A Are you into photography?
B Well, no. I just take photos of me and my friends.

2 Strategy plus *Really*

You can use *really* to make statements stronger and to make negative statements softer.

I'd really like to take a look sometime.

I don't really have much time.

Not really can also be a polite way to answer *no*.

About you

Pair work Ask and answer the questions. Give your own answers using *really* or *not really*.

1. Can you do anything artistic, like paint or draw?
2. Would you like to learn a new skill, like web design or . . . ?
3. Are you good at puzzles and crosswords?
4. Are you into computers?
5. Do you collect anything?
6. Do you like making things?

A *Can you do anything artistic, like paint or draw?*
B *Well, I really like drawing cartoons.* OR *Not really. I'm not very artistic.*

Sounds right p. 137

3 Listening and strategies Interesting hobbies

About you

Pair work Do you know anyone who does things like these? Which look interesting? Discuss with your partner.

☐ collecting baseball memorabilia

☐ editing videos

☐ fixing up motorcycles

☐ hiking

A *Are you interested in collecting things?*
B *Not really, but my sister collects teddy bears.*

B 🔊 **1.18** Listen to Bill, Sue, Jeff, and Lori talk about their hobbies. Number the pictures 1 to 4.

C 🔊 **1.18** Listen again. Who are the statements true for? Check (✓) the names. Sometimes more than one answer is possible.

	Bill	Sue	Jeff	Lori
1. I don't really have much time for my hobby.	☐	☐	☐	☐
2. I spend a lot of money on it.	☐	☐	☐	☐
3. I'm not really very good at it.	☐	☐	☐	☐
4. I make money on my hobby.	☐	☐	☐	☐

D **Pair work** Talk about one of your hobbies. Are the statements above true for you?

Free talk p. 129

1 Reading

A Look at the list of hobby groups on the online forum. Which ones are you interested in? Tell the class.

B Read the online forum. What problem does each person have? *Owl problem tiene cade pusona*

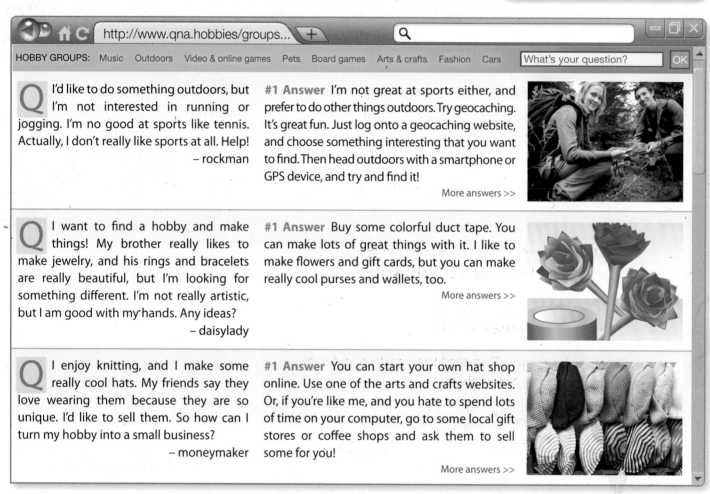

HOBBY GROUPS: Music   Outdoors   Video & online games   Pets   Board games   Arts & crafts   Fashion   Cars

Q I'd like to do something outdoors, but I'm not interested in running or jogging. I'm no good at sports like tennis. Actually, I don't really like sports at all. Help!
– rockman

#1 Answer I'm not great at sports either, and prefer to do other things outdoors. Try geocaching. It's great fun. Just log onto a geocaching website, and choose something interesting that you want to find. Then head outdoors with a smartphone or GPS device, and try and find it!

More answers >>

Q I want to find a hobby and make things! My brother really likes to make jewelry, and his rings and bracelets are really beautiful, but I'm looking for something different. I'm not really artistic, but I am good with my hands. Any ideas?
– daisylady

#1 Answer Buy some colorful duct tape. You can make lots of great things with it. I like to make flowers and gift cards, but you can make really cool purses and wallets, too.

More answers >>

Q I enjoy knitting, and I make some really cool hats. My friends say they love wearing them because they are so unique. I'd like to sell them. So how can I turn my hobby into a small business?
– moneymaker

#1 Answer You can start your own hat shop online. Use one of the arts and crafts websites. Or, if you're like me, and you hate to spend lots of time on your computer, go to some local gift stores or coffee shops and ask them to sell some for you!

More answers >>

C Read more answers to the questions above. Who are they for? Write the names.

1. **To:** _____ I like making jewelry, especially necklaces and earrings. I usually take them to a flea market and sell them there. It's easy to find flea markets in your area if you search online.

2. **To:** _Rockman_ More and more I hear that walking is one of the best exercises around. It's really good for you. And you don't have to walk fast. Just walk for 30 minutes or an hour at a normal speed.

3. **To:** _____ You could try pottery. You can make cups and bowls. You don't have to be creative.

4. **To:** _moneymaker_ There are some good classes. They teach you all about making money out of your hobby.

5. **To:** _____ How about creating your own greeting cards? People love getting handmade cards.

6. **To:** _Rockman_ Buy a bicycle. It's fun, it's good for you, and getting around is free!

About you **Pair work** What do you think of the answers to the questions on the message board? Can you think of a different answer for each question? Discuss with a partner.

2 Listening and speaking Favorite websites

A 🔊 1.19 Listen to Lisa and Joe talk about a website. What kind of website is it? Why does Joe like it?

B 🔊 1.19 Listen again. Circle the correct options to complete the sentences.

1. Joe checks the website **every day** / **every week**.
2. The website lists **50,000** / **5,000** places to hike.
3. Joe is reading an article about hiking **in the U.S.** / **in different countries**.
4. Joe wants to enter the competition to win a **tent** / **bike**.
5. Lisa prefers to cycle **indoors** / **outdoors**.

About you

Pair work Ask and answer the questions.

- What kinds of websites do you regularly use? What do you use them for?
- What are your favorite websites?
- Do you ever post comments on websites?
- Do you have your own website? What's it like?
- Do you ever enter competitions online?
- Do you prefer to read magazines online or in print?
- Do you ever read websites in English? Which ones?

3 Writing A message board

A Read the Help note. Then read the question and answer about hobbies. Circle the linking expressions.

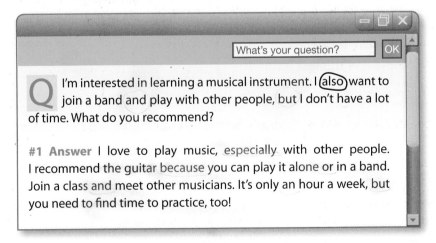

What's your question?   OK

Q I'm interested in learning a musical instrument. I (also) want to join a band and play with other people, but I don't have a lot of time. What do you recommend?

#1 Answer I love to play music, especially with other people. I recommend the guitar because you can play it alone or in a band. Join a class and meet other musicians. It's only an hour a week, but you need to find time to practice, too!

> **✎ Help note**
>
> **Linking ideas**
> - Add an idea:
>   *I enjoy knitting, **and** I make some really cool hats.*
>
>   *I **also** like making jewelry, **especially** bracelets.*
>
>   *I'm not interested in running **or** jogging.*
>
> - Contrast two ideas:
>   *I'm not good at sports, **but** I want to do something outdoors.*
>
> - Give a reason:
>   *My friends love wearing my hats **because** they are unique.*

About you

B Write a question about hobbies to post on a message board. Write an answer to three of your classmates' questions.

C **Group work** Read your question and classmates' answers to the group. Decide on the best idea.

Vocabulary notebook / I really like to sing!

Learning tip *Word chains*

Link new words together in word "chains."

In conversation

Favorite music

The top five types of music people talk about are:

1. rock   4. rap
2. classical   5. country
3. jazz

1 Complete the word chains using the words and expressions below.

bake cakes	play the guitar	skiing
listen to rock music	playing chess	writing poetry

I'm good at ▶ *skiing* and *playing chess* and *writing poetry* .

I don't like to ▶ *bake cakes* or *play the guitar* or *listen to rock music* .

2 Now complete the word chains with your own ideas.

I enjoy ▶ *eating* and *a eating* and *playing* .

I can't ▶ *cook* or *run* or *watch TV* .

I hate to ▶ *eat fruit* and *drink water* and *cook dinner* .

I'd like to ▶ *read the book* and *dance to bachata music* and *travel to Europe* .

3 Now make your own word chains using the expressions below.

I'm not interested in   I can   I like

I'm not interested in spelling chinese.
I can eat and drink and cook dinner
I like to dance and travel
I use money

On your own

Think of different things you are interested in. Can you link them together? Use the last letter of each word or expression to start the next word.

chessoccerockclimbinguit

✔ Can Do! Now I can . . .

✔ I can . . .	? I need to review how to . . .

- ☑ ask and answer questions about interests.
- ☑ talk about my taste in music.
- ☑ answer more than just *no* to be polite.
- ☑ use *really* and *not really* to strengthen or soften what I say.

- ☐ understand people talking about their hobbies.
- ☑ understand a conversation about a website.
- ☐ read an online forum.
- ☐ write questions and answers for an online forum.

Health

✓ Can Do! In this unit, you learn how to . . .

Lesson A
- Talk about exercise and how to stay healthy using the simple present and present continuous

Lesson B
- Discuss common health problems using *if* and *when*

Lesson C
- Comment and ask follow-up questions to encourage people to say more
- Use expressions like *Really?* and *Oh!* to show surprise

Lesson D
- Read an article about staying healthy
- Write questions and answers about health concerns

Before you begin . . .

Which of these things do you do to stay healthy? What else can you do?

1. Eat plenty of fruits and vegetables.
2. Go to the gym and work out.
3. Play sports.
4. Take regular breaks to cope with stress.
5. Sleep at least seven hours a night.
6. Get a checkup once a year.

Are you doing anything to stay **healthy**?

"Well, I generally don't eat a lot of junk food, and I don't eat red meat at all. And right now I'm doing karate. It's getting me in shape quick."
—Brian Jones

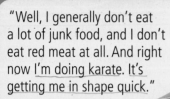

"Um . . . right now I'm trying to lose weight before my school reunion, so I'm drinking these diet drinks for dinner."
—Carmen Sanchez

"Not really. I kind of eat everything I want. I don't do anything to stay in shape. I'm just lucky, I guess."
—Lisa da Silva

"Well, I walk everywhere I go because I don't have a car, so I think I get enough exercise."
—Mei-ling Yu

"Um . . . to be honest, I'm not doing anything right now. I'm studying for exams this month, so I'm eating a lot of snacks, and I'm not getting any exercise at all."
—Michael Evans

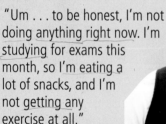

"Yeah, we exercise six days a week. We go swimming every other day, and in between we go to the gym. And once in a while, we go hiking."
—The Parks

1 Getting started

A 🔊 1.20 Listen to the on-the-street interviews. Who do you think has a healthy lifestyle? Why?

Figure it out Complete these sentences with a simple present or present continuous verb. Use the interviews to help you. Are the sentences true for you? Tell a partner.

1. I generally _____ (not eat) junk food.
2. I usually _____ (get) enough exercise.
3. We usually _____ (go) to the gym every other day.
4. I _____ (eat) a lot of snacks this month.
5. These days I _____ (not get) any exercise at all.
6. Right now I _____ (try) to get in shape.

2 Grammar Simple present and present continuous ◀)) 1.21

Extra practice p. 142

★ **Use the simple present to talk about "all the time"** (*usually* or *generally*) and routines.
How **do** you **stay** in shape?
  I **walk** everywhere. I **don't have** a car.

  Does she **get** regular exercise?
    Yes, she **does**. She **exercises** six days a week.
    No, she **doesn't**. She **doesn't exercise** at all.

Use the present continuous to talk about "now" (*these days*, *this month*) and temporary events.
What sports **are** you **playing** these days?
  I**'m doing** karate. It**'s getting** me in shape.

  Is she **trying** to lose weight?
    Yes, she **is**. She**'s drinking** diet drinks.
    No, she**'s not**. She**'s not trying** to lose weight.

In conversation

The simple present is about six times more frequent than the present continuous and even more frequent with *like*, *love*, *know*, *need*, and *want*.

X Common errors

Don't forget to use *be* in the present continuous.
I'm doing karate.
(NOT ~~I doing~~ *karate*.)

A Complete the conversations with the simple present or present continuous. Then practice with a partner.

1. A How _____do_____ you _____cope_____ (cope) with stress?
   _____ you _____ (get) stressed a lot?

   B Well, generally I _____ (not feel) stressed, but we _____ (work) long hours this month. So my co-workers and I _____ (take) a meditation class right now. It's great. Meditation really _____relaxes_____ (relax) you.

2. A _____ you _____ (like) to play sports?

   B Not really, but my wife and I _____ (enjoy) swimming. We usually _____ (go) to the pool together in the summer. Now that it's winter, I _____ (not swim) at all. But my wife _____ (go) every day, even when it's cold.

3. A _____ your family _____ (do) anything new to stay healthy?

   B Actually, yeah. We _____ (try) to eat a balanced diet. I mean, everybody in the family _____loves_____ (love) fast food, but right now, we _____ (cook) healthy meals. It's not easy because my husband _____ (not like) vegetables and things like that.

About you Pair work Ask and answer the questions above. Give your own answers.

3 Listening and speaking Unhealthy habits

A ◀)) 1.22 Try to guess what unhealthy habit each person is talking about. Then listen and complete the sentences.

1. Ian says he eats a lot of _____ , but he wants to cut down on it.
2. Kaylie wants to give up _____ , but she can't.
3. Martin's mom says Martin spends too much time _____ .
4. Silvia's husband says she's not _____ enough these days.

B ◀)) 1.23 Listen again to the last thing each person says. Do you agree? Why or why not? Tell the class.

About you Pair work Do you have any of the same unhealthy habits? What other unhealthy habits do you have? Tell your partner.

1 Building vocabulary

A 🔊 1.24 Listen and say the sentences. Do you have any of these problems right now?

I have **a fever**. I think I'm getting **the flu**.

I have **a bad cough**. I**'m coughing** a lot.

I have **a stomachache**. I often get stomachaches.

I have **a toothache**.

I hardly ever get **headaches**, but I have one now.

I have **a cold** and **a sore throat**. I get a lot of colds.

I feel **sick**. I often get sick when I eat shellfish.

I have **allergies**. I'm **sneezing** all the time, and my eyes itch.

Word sort Complete the chart with the words above. Add other ideas. Then compare with a partner.

I never . . .	I hardly ever . . .	I sometimes . . .	I often . . .
get colds		have a runny nose	sneeze

"I never get colds. But sometimes I have a runny nose. I think I have allergies."

📓 **Vocabulary notebook** p. 30

2 Speaking naturally Contrasts

A *What's the matter? Do you have a cold?*
B *No, I have a headache. I feel terrible.*
A *That's too bad. I hope you feel better.*
B *Thanks.*

A 🔊 1.25 Listen and repeat the conversation above. Notice how stress shows the contrast between *headache* and *cold*, and between *better* and *terrible*.

B **Pair work** Practice the conversation. Then practice again using different health problems.

3 Building language

A 🔊 1.26 **Listen. What does Nora want to make for Ken? Practice the conversation.**

Ken Hello?

Nora Hi, Ken. How are you feeling?

Ken Awful. I still have this terrible cold.

Nora That's too bad. Are you taking anything for it?

Ken Just some cold medicine.

Nora Hmm. I never take that stuff when I have a cold. But if I get a really bad cold, I drink hot vinegar with honey. I can make you some.

Ken Oh, no thanks! I don't feel *that* bad!

Figure it out **Unscramble the sentences below. Are the sentences true for you?**

1. I take / a cold / when / medicine / I have

    _____ .

2. I make / I have / hot tea with lemon / If / the flu,

    _____ .

4 Grammar Joining clauses with *if* and *when* 🔊 1.27

Extra practice p. 142

What do you take **when** you have a cold?	What do you do **if** you get a really bad cold?
I don't take anything **when** I have a cold.	I drink hot vinegar with honey **if** I get a really bad cold.
When I have a cold, I don't take anything.	**If** I get a really bad cold, I drink hot vinegar with honey.

A **Complete the questions with *if you* followed by the correct expressions from the box.**

feel run down	get a toothache	have a bad cough	have a runny nose
feel sore	get an upset stomach	have a headache	✓have a sore throat

1. Do you gargle salt water __*if you have a sore throat*__ ?
2. _____ after a meal, do you drink herbal tea?
3. What do you do _____ and you have no energy?
4. Do you stretch _____ after exercising?
5. _____ and itchy eyes, do you take allergy medicine?
6. _____ , do you go to the dentist right away?
7. What do you do _____ ? Do you suck on a cough drop?
8. What do you do __have a headache__ ? Do you take aspirin?

About you **Pair work Ask and answer the questions above. Use *when* in your answers.**

A *Do you gargle salt water if you have a sore throat?*

B *Actually, when I have a sore throat, I drink hot tea with honey. Do you take anything?*

About you **Do you and your partner do any of the same things in the situations above? Tell the class.**

🔊 **Sounds right** p. 137

1 Conversation strategy Encouraging people to talk

A Why do people get tired? Brainstorm ideas and make a list.

"People often feel tired when they have a cold."

B 🔊 1.28 Listen. Why is Stan tired?

Stan	I'm so tired.
Yuki	Really? How come?
Stan	Well, I'm working two jobs this semester, so I'm getting up at, like, 5:30 to study.
Yuki	You're kidding! Two jobs? Wow.
Stan	Yeah. Just for a couple of months. I'm working in a supermarket after class, and then I have my regular job at the restaurant till 11:00.
Yuki	Oh, that's late. So, what time do you go to bed?
Stan	About 1:00 . . . 1:30.
Yuki	Gosh. So you're only getting about four hours' sleep? That's not much.

C Notice how Yuki encourages Stan to continue talking. She comments on what Stan says and asks follow-up questions. Find examples in the conversation.

"I'm so tired."
"Really? How come?"

D Match each sentence with an appropriate reply. Then practice with a partner.

1. I often stay up until 2:00 or 3:00 a.m. __e__
2. I love sleeping late on weekends. _____
3. I often take a nap during my lunch break. _____
4. I only sleep about five hours a night. _____
5. I sometimes fall asleep in lectures. _____
6. I usually go to bed early during the week. _____

a. You do? Does the professor notice?
b. That's good. Do you wake up early, too?
c. That's not much. Do you get tired during the day?
d. At work? How long do you sleep?
e. Really? What do you do all night?
f. Me too. What time do you get up on Sundays?

About you **Pair work** Student A: Tell a partner about your sleep habits. Use the ideas above.
Student B: Respond with comments and questions. Then change roles.

A I usually stay up until about 11:00, 11:30 during the week.
B Really? That's not too late. Do you stay up late on weekends?
A Not really. I go to bed about the same time.

2 Strategy plus Showing surprise

Use expressions like these to show surprise in informal conversations:

Oh!	*Gosh!*
Really?	*Oh, my gosh!*
Wow!	*You're kidding!*
Oh, wow!	*Are you serious?*
No way!	*No!*

In formal conversations, use *Oh!* or *Really?*

I'm working two jobs this semester.

You're kidding! Two jobs? Wow.

In conversation

Oh and *Really* are in the top 50 words. *Wow* and *Gosh* are in the top 500.

A 🔊 **1.29** **Listen and write the expressions you hear. Then practice with a partner.**

1. A I never hear my alarm clock.
   B _____Really_____? So how do you wake up?

2. A I often fall asleep on the subway.
   B _You're kidding_! Do you ever miss your stop?

3. A I have the same dream every night.
   B _No way_! Every single night?

4. A I can't sleep if it's light.
   B _Gosh_! Do you wear an eye mask?

5. A I often sleep for 12 or 13 hours.
   B _Are you serious_? Is that only on weekends?

6. A I can't fall asleep without music.
   B _____! What do you listen to?

About you 🔊 **1.30** **Listen to the comments again. Respond with a different expression to show surprise and add your own question. Then practice with a partner.**

3 Strategies Sweet dreams

About you **up work** **Discuss the questions about sleep habits. What do you have in common? Encourage your classmates to talk by commenting and asking follow-up questions.**

- What do you do if you can't sleep?
- Do you ever wake up during the night?
- Are you tired today? If so, why?
- Do you ever take naps during the daytime?

- Do you ever have vivid dreams or nightmares?
- Do you remember your dreams?
- Do you snore or talk in your sleep?
- Do you ever fall asleep in front of the TV?

   A *What do you do if you can't sleep?*
   B *Well, if I wake up and can't get back to sleep, I usually get up and play a video game.*
   C *You're kidding! So do you go back to bed after that?*

Free talk p. 130

1 Reading

A What can you do to stay healthy? How many ideas can you think of in 30 seconds? Make a list.

B Read the article. Which of your ideas are mentioned? What other ideas does it suggest?

Rethink Your Way to Great Health

Let's face it: many of us are not too healthy. We often take an "all or nothing" approach to health. If we can't exercise every day, follow a healthy diet, or manage our stress levels, then we give up and do nothing. However, looking after our health doesn't have to take a lot of time and effort. It just takes a little thought. Follow these simple ideas and rethink your way to better health!

First, get moving. How much are you exercising these days? Not a lot? Research shows not exercising is really bad for your health. If you can't afford to go to the gym, go running. Skip the elevator and take the stairs; don't take the bus or train all the way – walk. Or, try exercising while you watch TV.

Second, don't forget to take a break from work sometimes. Our bodies can't go, go, go all day! We need to take regular breaks. If work is stressing you out, take a few deep breaths in between tasks. Try a relaxation technique, like meditation, or take a relaxing ten-minute walk.

Next, be sure to make good food choices. When you get stressed, do you reach for a cookie? Don't snack on junk food. Plan ahead and keep healthy snacks like fruit or nuts nearby. When you go shopping, buy only healthy foods for your next meal. If you have to order fast food, choose something light, go easy on the dressings, and add a healthy side dish like a salad or fruit.

Finally, remember to sleep well. Don't fall asleep with the TV on. When you go to bed, make sure your room is quiet, cool, and dark. Research shows it's the best way to get a good night's sleep.

With simple changes like these, you can rethink your way to great health, one choice at a time. It's up to you!

C Read the article again. Answer the questions. Then compare with a partner.

1. Why do some people stop exercising and eating well?
2. What relaxation technique does the article mention?
3. What are some examples of healthy snacks from the article?
4. What healthy options do you have when you eat fast food?
5. What kinds of things can you do to get more exercise?
6. What can help you get a good night's sleep?

About you **Pair work** Discuss the suggestions in the article. Do you follow any of them? If yes, which ones? If no, say why not.

2 Listening Coping with stress

A What do you do to cope with stress? Do you do any of these things? Tell a partner.

_____ _____ _____ _____

B 🔊 1.31 Listen to four people talk about how they cope with stress. Number the pictures 1 to 4.

C 🔊 1.32 Listen again. What else do they do when they're feeling stressed? Write the activity under the picture.

3 Writing That's great advice!

A Read the Help note and the posts on a social networking site. Add commas to the *if* and *when* clauses in the two suggestions.

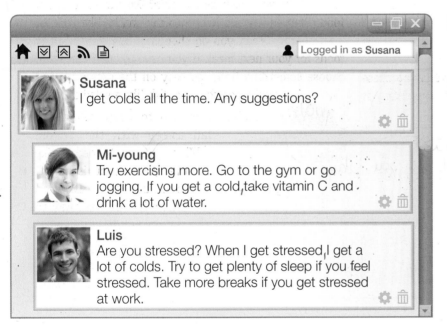

Logged in as **Susana**

Susana
I get colds all the time. Any suggestions?

Mi-young
Try exercising more. Go to the gym or go jogging. If you get a cold, take vitamin C and drink a lot of water.

Luis
Are you stressed? When I get stressed, I get a lot of colds. Try to get plenty of sleep if you feel stressed. Take more breaks if you get stressed at work.

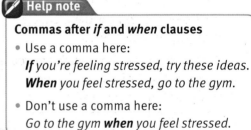

Help note

Commas after *if* and *when* clauses
- Use a comma here:
  If you're feeling stressed, try these ideas.
  When you feel stressed, go to the gym.
- Don't use a comma here:
  Go to the gym when you feel stressed.

B Write your own suggestion to Susana. Then compare with a partner.

About you **Group work** Write a question about your health on a piece of paper. Use the ideas below to help you. Then exchange papers. Write a reply to each person.

Marla
I'm not sleeping at night. Help!

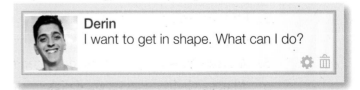

Derin
I want to get in shape. What can I do?

About you **Group work** Read the replies. Which suggestion(s) would you like to try? Tell the group.

Learning tip *Learning words together*

When you learn a new word or expression, write down other words you can use with it.

1 Complete these expressions. Use the words in the box.

a break   better   home   in bed   medicine   sick

feel	stay	take

2 Which of these verbs can you use with the words and expressions in the chart? Complete the chart. You can use some verbs more than once.

be   do   feel   get   go (to)   have   see   stay   take

be, feel, get	sick		exercise		a vacation
	allergies		a headache		a cough
	a checkup		home		healthy
	stressed		in shape		a doctor

 On your own

Go to a drugstore and look at different medicines. What health problems are they for? Can you remember the names of the health problems in English?

It's for a cough.

Can Do! Now I can . . .

✓ I can . . .	? I need to review how to . . .

☐ talk about exercise and how to stay healthy.

☐ discuss common health problems.

☐ say what I do when I have a health problem.

☐ keep a conversation going.

☐ show surprise in formal and informal conversations.

☐ understand people talking about unhealthy habits.

☐ understand conversations about coping with stress.

☐ read an article about how to stay healthy.

☐ write questions and answers about health concerns.

2 Grammar Future with *be going to*; indirect objects ◀)) 2.03

Extra practice p. 143

be going to

I'm	**going to** buy something special.
You're	**going to** get a present.
She's	**going to** be 50.
We're	**going to** send some flowers.
They're	**going to** have a party.

What **are** you **going to** do for your birthday?
  I'**m not going to** do anything special.

Are you **going to** have a party?
  Yes, we **are**. We'**re going to** invite all our friends.
  No, we'**re not**. We'**re not going to** do much.

Indirect objects

buy / give / send **someone** something
I'm going to buy **my mother** something special.
Alicia isn't going to give **Dave** anything.
Let's send **Mom and Dad** some flowers.

Indirect object pronouns

me, you, him, her, us, them
I'm going to buy **her** something special.
Alicia isn't going to give **him** anything.
Let's send **them** some flowers.

A Write questions with *be going to* using the prompts given. Then write your own answers using indirect object pronouns where necessary.

1. you / do anything special / for your next birthday?
   Are you going to do anything special for your next birthday?
   Actually, my friends are going to buy me dinner.

2. your parents / buy / you / something nice / on your next birthday?
   Are you parents going to buy you something nice on your next birthday?

3. What / you / get / your friends / for their birthdays?
   What are you going to get yours/friends for their birthdays?

4. you and your classmates / send / your teacher / a birthday card?
   Are you and your classmates going to send your teacher a birthday card?

5. When are your parents' birthdays? What gifts / you / buy?
   What gifts are you going to buy him? what/what gifts are you going to buy?

6. What / you / buy / your parents / for their anniversary?
   What are you want to buy your parents for their anniversary?

About you **Pair work** Ask and answer the questions.

A *Are you going to do anything special for your next birthday?*

B *Well, actually, I'm going to be 21, so I'm going to have a big party.*

3 Speaking naturally *going to*

> What are you **going to** do tonight? Are you **going to** go to the movies? I'm **going to** stay home.

A ◀)) 2.04 Listen and repeat the sentences above. Notice the ways of saying *going to*.

About you ◀)) 2.05 Listen and complete the sentences with the missing words. Then ask a partner the questions.

1. Are you *going to send* anyone flowers this year?
2. Are you _____ any expensive gifts this year?
3. Are you _____ any cards this month?
4. Are you _____ anyone's birthday this month?
5. Who are you _____ your next birthday with?

  A *Are you going to send anyone flowers this year?*

  B *Yeah, I'm going to send my mom flowers on Mother's Day.*

35

1 Building vocabulary

Word sort What do people do on these special days? Find two expressions from the box for each event. What else do people do? Add ideas.

blow out candles on a cake	go out for a romantic dinner	✓ shout "Happy New Year"
exchange rings	go to see fireworks	sing "Happy Birthday"
give someone chocolates	go trick-or-treating	wear a cap and gown
get a degree or diploma	have a reception	wear a costume

1

New Year's Eve
shout "Happy New Year"
_____
_____

2

Valentine's Day
_____
_____
_____

3

birthday
_____
_____
_____

4

graduation day
_____
_____
_____

5

Halloween
_____
_____
_____

6

wedding day
_____
_____
_____

Vocabulary notebook p. 42

About you **B Pair work** Talk about special days or events you are going to celebrate this year. When are they? How are you going to celebrate them?

A *What are you going to do on New Year's Eve?*
B *I'm going to go to a New Year's Eve party with some friends.*

Sounds right p. 137

2 Building language

A 🔊 **2.06 Listen to Marcella's phone message. What are her plans for tomorrow night?**

Voice mail   Hi. This is Laurie. Please leave a message after the beep. Thanks for calling.

Marcella   Hi, Laurie. This is Marcella. Listen, what are you doing tomorrow night? A group of us are going out for dinner and then to a big New Year's Eve party. Do you want to come? We're meeting at the restaurant at 8:30, and we're probably going to go to the party around 11:00. It's going to be a lot of fun. So call me back, OK? Oh, and by the way, they say it's going to snow tomorrow, so be careful. Bye.

Figure it out   Find Marcella's plans and the weather prediction. What verb forms does she use?

3 Grammar   Present continuous for the future; *be going to* 🔊 **2.07**

Extra practice p. 143

You can use the present continuous or *be going to* to talk about plans.
The present continuous is often used for plans with specific times or places.

What **are** you **doing** for New Year's Eve?
  We**'re going to** The Sea Grill for dinner.
  We**'re meeting** friends there at 8:30.

What **are** you **going to do** for New Year's Eve?
  We**'re going to go** somewhere for dinner.
  We**'re going to meet** some friends at a restaurant.

You can also use *be going to* for predictions.
It**'s going to be** fun. (NOT It's being fun.)
It**'s going to snow** tomorrow. (NOT It's snowing tomorrow.)

✗ Common errors

Remember to use a form of *be* with *going to* and the present continuous.

We're going to meet some friends.
(NOT ~~We going~~ to meet . . .)

We're meeting some friends.
(NOT ~~We meeting~~ . . .)

A Match each plan with a prediction. Then role-play with a partner. Ask follow-up questions.

1. I think my parents are going to get me something special for graduation. _h_
2. My neighbors are going trick-or-treating on Halloween. _____
3. My best friend's getting married in May. _____
4. My sister's graduating from law school soon. _____
5. I'm going to get my dad a tie for his birthday. _____
6. My best friend and I are going to Paris next month. _____
7. My sister's having a baby next month. _____
8. My mom's going to retire next year. _____

a. I think he's going to love it.
b. She's going to be a great lawyer.
c. It's going to be a fun wedding.
d. We're going to have a great time.
e. I think it's going to be a boy.
f. It's going to rain, but they don't care.
g. She's going to love not going to work.
h. Or they're going to give me some money.

About you   Pair work Find out about each other's plans for next weekend.

A What are you doing next weekend?
B Well, I'm meeting a friend, and we're going to go roller-skating.

1 Conversation strategy "Vague" expressions

A What kinds of things do people do at fiestas and festivals? Make a list.

B 🔊 2.08 Listen. What happens during the fiesta?

Ray Are you going to the fiesta this weekend?

Tina I don't know. It depends. What is it exactly?

Ray Well, it's just, um . . . it's a festival. It's lots of parades and stuff like that. Everybody gets dressed up, you know . . .

Tina You mean in costumes?

Ray Yeah. There are hundreds of cute little kids in purple and silver outfits with makeup and everything. . . .

Tina Uh-huh. Uh, I'm not big on parades.

Ray And there's good food. You can get all kinds of tacos and things. Do you want to go?

Tina Hmm. Well, maybe.

C **Notice** how Ray uses "vague" expressions like these. He doesn't need to give Tina a complete list. Find examples in the conversation.

> *and stuff (like that)*
> *and things (like that)*
> *and everything*

> 💬 **In conversation**
> People use *and stuff* in very informal situations.
>
> *and stuff* ▮▮▮ *and things* ▮

D Find the vague expressions in these conversations. What do they mean? Choose two ideas from the box for each one.

| anniversaries | concerts | dancing | holidays | sing "Happy Birthday" |
| candles | cultural events | folk songs | ✓ see old friends | spend time at home |

1. A What are you doing for spring break?
   B I'm going home. I really want to see my family (and everything.) *see old friends*

2. A Do you usually go to a restaurant to celebrate birthdays and stuff?
   B Yeah, we know a nice place. They bring out cakes and everything.

3. A Are you into traditional music and stuff like that?
   B Yeah, we have a lot of music festivals and things like that around here.

About you **Pair work** Ask and answer the questions. Give your own answers.

38

2 Strategy plus "Vague" responses

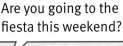

You can use responses
like these if you're not
sure about your answer:

I don't know.
I'm not sure.
Maybe.
It depends.

💬 **In conversation**

I don't know is the most
common of these responses.

I don't know. It depends.
What is it exactly?

Are you going to the
fiesta this weekend?

A Match each question with two responses. Then practice with
a partner.

1. ˙Are you going to go to any festivals this year? __a__ ____
2. My friend's having a party this weekend. Do you want to go? ____ ____
3. Are we going to plan an end-of-year party after the last class? ____ ____
4. I have an extra ticket for a concert tonight. Do you want it? ____ ____

a. I'm not sure. There's a film festival in March.

b. Maybe. Let's talk to the teacher about it.

c. It depends. When is it? This Saturday?

d. I don't know. I think I'm working all weekend.

e. I'm not sure. I'm feeling kind of tired.

f. It depends. Who's playing?

g. I don't know. It sounds like a lot of work.

h. Maybe. I'd like to go to a folk festival.

About you **Pair work** Ask and answer the questions. Give your own information.

3 Listening and strategies Celebrations around the world

A 🔊 **2.09** Look at the pictures of two festivals. What's happening? Then listen and answer
the questions about each festival.

1. Which country celebrates the festival?
2. When is it?
3. How do people celebrate?
4. Do they eat any special foods?
5. Why do they celebrate?

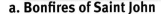

a. Bonfires of Saint John　　**b. The Festival of Colors**

About you **Pair work** Student A: Choose a festival you know. Student B: Ask your partner the questions above.
Can you guess the festival? Are you going to celebrate it?

A So, which country celebrates the festival and when is it?

B Well, it depends. It's usually in February and a lot of people celebrate it around the world.
People see fireworks and stuff.

Free talk p. 130

1 Reading

A What do people in your country do for these events?

They exchange rings.

weddings   birthdays   New Year's Eve

B Read the article. Which traditions are similar to the ones in your country? Which are different?

> **Reading tip**
> Look at the photos. They can sometimes help you with the vocabulary in an article.

Let's celebrate!

Although people around the world celebrate many of the same events, they sometimes celebrate these special days quite differently. We found some interesting – and unique – traditions for celebrating New Year's Eve, birthdays, and weddings.

Are these newlyweds going to have good luck?

BIRTHDAYS

In China, there's an interesting birthday tradition for infants. A baby is one year old on the day he or she is born. One year later, friends and relatives get together for the baby's second birthday. They put several objects in front of the baby, such as some money, a doll, and a book. If the baby picks up the money, it means he or she is going to be wealthy. Reaching for the book means the baby is going to be a teacher, and picking up the doll means the baby is going to have a lot of children one day.

What is the new year going to bring?

What's this baby's future?

NEW YEAR'S EVE

In Mexico, people celebrate the start of the new year by getting together with friends and family. On New Year's Eve, they have a special dinner. Then, when the clock strikes midnight, everyone starts eating grapes – one for each month of the next year. A sweet grape means the month is going to be a good one. If a grape is sour, then the month is not going to be so good.

WEDDINGS

Weddings around the world have different traditions, and Venezuela is no exception. Of course, during a wedding ceremony, couples promise that they will always love and take care of each other. However, in Venezuela, the bride and groom don't always say their promises – sometimes they sing them. Later, during the reception, the bride and groom sneak away. If no one sees them leave, it means they are going to have good luck in their marriage. And that seems to be something that all these traditions have in common – they are all meant to bring good luck.

C Read the article again. Are the sentences true or false? Check (✓) *True* (T) or *False* (F).

		T	F
1.	In Mexico, people eat grapes at a special dinner.	☐	☐
2.	If you eat a sweet grape on New Year's Eve, it means that the year ahead is going to be good.	☐	☐
3.	In China, the family gets together on the day the baby is born.	☐	☐
4.	If the baby picks up a doll, it means he or she is going to have a lot of brothers and sisters.	☐	☐
5.	In Venezuela, the bride and groom can sing their promises to love each other.	☐	☐
6.	If they don't go to the reception, it means they will have good luck in their marriage.	☐	☐

About you D Group work Discuss these questions about traditions.

- What traditions do you have for wedding receptions?
- Which birthdays are extra special? How do people celebrate them?
- What traditions do you have for New Year's Day? What brings good luck for the new year?

2 Listening and writing Congratulations!

A ◀)) 2.10 Listen to these people talk about their invitations to the events below. Complete the information.

Subject: Elaine's housewarming party
From: Elaine Collins (elaine@cup.org)

Hi Simon and Julie,
My new apartment is ready and I'm finally having a housewarming party! It's on Saturday, _____ at _____ p.m. My new address is 1452 E. Mulberry St. By the way, Sally is going to bring some _____ . Simon, can you make some of your special _____ ? Thanks!
See you,
Elaine

In celebration of their _____ wedding anniversary, Iris and Derek invite you to dinner on _____ , _____ , at _____ p.m. at The French Restaurant.

Dear John and Jessie,
Hope you can make it to the dinner. There's going to be _____ and _____ afterward. We look forward to seeing you both.
Best regards, Iris and Derek

B Read the Help note. Then find the expressions in the invitations above and circle them.

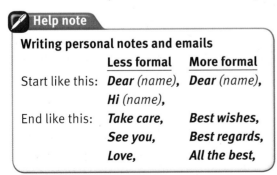

Help note

Writing personal notes and emails

	Less formal	More formal
Start like this:	*Dear (name),* *Hi (name),*	*Dear (name),*
End like this:	*Take care,* *See you,* *Love,*	*Best wishes,* *Best regards,* *All the best,*

About you Invite a partner to a special event. Write an invitation and add a personal note. Then exchange invitations with your partner. Write a response.

Vocabulary notebook / Calendars

Learning tip *Linking events with dates*

You can write down some of your new vocabulary on a calendar.
It's a useful way to learn the names of special events and celebrations.

1 Complete the calendar with words from the box.

anniversary	dinner	February	flowers	graduation	May	September	Valentine's
card	Eve	fireworks	gown	Halloween	November	vacation	

January	11th – Mom's birthday. Buy her _____ and a cake.
_____	14th – _____ Day!
March	23rd – Suzanne's birthday. Go out for _____ .
April	1st – April Fool's Day
_____	4th – My birthday!
June	2nd – End of exams 21st – School _____ . Rent a cap and _____ .

July	1st – Summer _____ starts. 22nd – Dad's 65th birthday.
August	16th – Summer party and _____ at night.
_____	10th – Jack and Betty's wedding _____ . Send them a _____ .
October	31st – _____ .
_____	28th – Family reunion for Thanksgiving.
December	31st – New Year's _____ party.

2 Now make your own calendar. Note important dates and plans in your year.

 On your own

Buy a wall calendar. Each month, circle your important dates and write your appointments and events in English.

✓ **Can Do!** **Now I can . . .**

✓ I can . . .	? I need to review how to . . .

- ☐ talk about birthdays, celebrations, and holidays.
- ☐ discuss future plans and make predictions.
- ☐ talk about gift giving.
- ☐ describe how I celebrate special days and holidays.
- ☐ use "vague" expressions like *and everything*.

- ☐ give vague responses like *It depends*.
- ☐ understand conversations about festivals.
- ☐ understand conversations about parties.
- ☐ read an article about world traditions.
- ☐ write an invitation to a special event.

Growing up

☑ Can Do! In this unit, you learn how to . . .

Lesson A
- Talk about growing up and your family background using the simple past

Lesson B
- Talk about school subjects people studied using *most (of)*, *a few (of)*, etc.

Lesson C
- Correct things you say with expressions like *Well*, *Actually*, and *No, wait*
- Use *I mean* to correct a word or name

Lesson D
- Read an interview with someone about his teenage years
- Write answers to interview questions

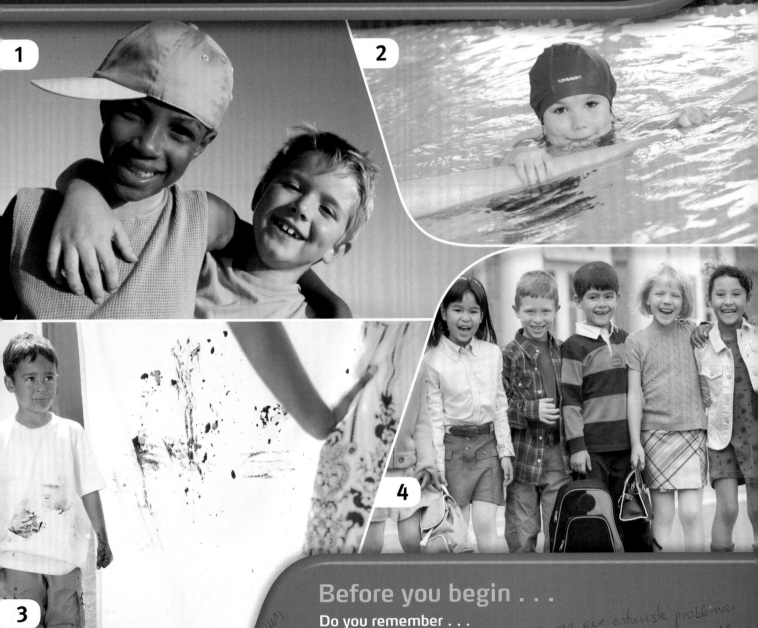

1

2

3

4

Before you begin . . .

Do you remember . . .

- your first close friend?
- learning to swim?
- a time you got into <u>trouble</u>?
- your first day of school?

Do you have other memories like these?

43

Ramon   That's a great baseball shirt, Ling. Are you from Seattle?

Ling   Um, kind of. I lived there, but I wasn't born there.

Ramon   Oh, yeah? Where were you born?

Ling   In São Paulo, actually.

Ramon   São Paulo? Brazil?

Ling   Yeah. My parents were born in Hong Kong, but they moved to São Paulo just before I was born.

Ramon   Wow. How long did you live there?

Ling   Until I was six. Then we moved to the U.S.

Ramon   To Seattle?

Ling   Yeah. We lived there for ten years, and we came here to San Francisco about three years ago.

Ramon   Huh. So did you grow up bilingual?

Ling   Well, we always spoke Chinese at home. I couldn't speak English until I went to school. And actually, I can still speak a little Portuguese.

1 Getting started

A Complete the two sentences below. Then tell the class.

I was born in _____ . I grew up in _____ .

B 🔊 **2.11** Listen. Where was Ling born? Where does she live now? Practice the conversation.

Figure it out

Circle the correct words to complete the sentences. Use the conversation above to help you.

1. Ling's parents **born / were born** in Hong Kong.

2. Ling lived in São Paulo **for / until** six years.

3. Ling moved to Seattle **when / until** she was six.

4. Ling's family moved to San Francisco three years **long / ago**.

2 Grammar *be born*; simple past (review); time expressions ◀)) 2.12

Extra practice p. 144

Where **were** you **born**?
I **was born** in São Paulo.
I **wasn't born** in Seattle.

Where **were** your parents **born**?
They **were born** in Hong Kong.
They **weren't born** in the U.S.

How long did you live in São Paulo?
We lived there **until** I was six. **From** 1995 **to** 2001.
We didn't leave **until** 2001. **Then** we came to the U.S.

When did they come here?
They came here about **three years ago**.
They came **when** Ling was sixteen.

Did you live there **for a long time**?
Yes, (I did). I lived there **for six years**.
No, (I didn't). I didn't live there **long**.

Did she move here **last year**?
Yes, (she did). She moved **in May**.
No, (she didn't). She moved **in 2011**.

A ◀)) 2.13 **Complete the conversations with the verbs given. Circle the correct words. Then listen and check.**

Saying years

1906 = "Nineteen oh-six"
1988 = "Nineteen eighty-eight"
2007 = "Two thousand (and) seven"
2015 = "Twenty fifteen"

1. A Where __*was*__ your mother __*born*__ (be born)?
   _____ your father _____ (be born) there, too?

   B My parents _____ (be born) in Vancouver (**in**)/ **to** 1945.

✗ Common errors

Don't confuse *before* and *ago*.

We moved here **six years ago**.
(NOT *We moved here* ~~before six years~~.
OR *We moved here* ~~six years before~~.)

2. A Where _____ you _____ (live) when you were young? _____ you _____ (grow up) in a big city?

   B Actually, I _____ (grow up) in Seattle. We _____ (stay) there **from** / **until** I started high school.

3. A Who _____ (be) your best friend in school? How long _____ (be) you friends?

   B Well, my best friend _____ (be) Jane. We _____ (be) friends **for** / **from** a long time.

4. A _____ you and your best friend ever _____ (argue)? What _____ you _____ (fight) about?

   B We _____ (not / fight) a lot. But one time we _____ (not / talk) **for** / **until** three weeks.

5. A Who took care of you **ago** / **when** you _____ (be) little? _____ your mother _____ (have) a job?

   B My mother _____ (work), so no one _____ (be) home **when** / **then** I _____ (get) home from school. I _____ (go) to a neighbor's house. But I _____ (not / be) there **long** / **until**.

6. A _____ you ever _____ (get) in trouble? What _____ you _____ (do)?

   B Oh, I _____ (get) in big trouble one time **when** / **then** I was seven. My mom _____ (be) mad at me **for** / **from** days! **Then** / **When** I _____ (make) her a card saying, "Sorry."

About you **Pair work** Practice the conversations. Then take turns asking the questions again. Give your own answers.

3 Speaking naturally *did you*

Where **did you** *go on vacation?*   *What* **did you** *do?*   **Did you** *have fun?*

A ◀)) 2.14 **Listen and repeat the questions above. Notice the ways of saying *did you*.**

About you ◀)) 2.15 **Listen and complete the questions about childhood vacations. Then ask and answer the questions with a partner.**

1. Did you _____ ?
2. Where did you _____ ?
3. How long did you _____ ?
4. Who did you _____ ?
5. Did you _____ ?
6. What did you _____ ?

1 Building language

A 🔊 2.16 Listen. What languages did these people study in school?

"All the students in my high school had to take English — it was required. And I needed English to get into my university. Some people need it for their jobs as well."

—Mi-chung, Seoul

"Well, years ago, most people learned Russian, and only a few people took English. I studied both."

—Karina, Prague

"I took Spanish last year, and most of my friends did, too. But only a few of us speak it well. Um, there are a lot of Spanish speakers around here, so it's kind of useful."

—Brad, Los Angeles

"A lot of my classmates dropped French after ninth grade. Almost all of them — except me. But then, later, some of them had to take evening classes because they needed it for work."

—Femi, Lagos

Figure it out Circle the correct expression to complete the sentences. Are they true for your friends?

1. **Most / Most of** people like English.
2. **Most / Most of** my friends study English.
3. **Some / Some of** them are fluent in English.
4. **A few / A few of** people study two languages.

2 Grammar Determiners 🔊 2.17

Extra practice p. 144

General (*students, Canadians*)	Specific (*the students in my class, my friends*)	With pronouns
All children learn a language.	**All (of)** the children in my town take English.	**All of them . . .**
Most Canadians need French.	**Most of** the people in my office know French.	**Most of us . . .**
Some students take Spanish.	**Some of** the students in my class take Greek.	**Some of us . . .**
A few people are good at Latin.	**A few of** my classmates got As.	**A few of them . . .**
No students like exams.	**None of** my friends failed the exams.	**None of them . . .**
But		
A lot of people speak English well.	**A lot of** the people in this city speak English.	**A lot of them . . .**

About you Make true sentences using determiners. Then compare with a partner.

1. _____ my friends studied English in middle school.
   _____ middle school students take English.
2. Today, _____ employees need a second language for their jobs.
   _____ companies require English skills to get a job.
3. _____ my friends speak two languages.
   _____ them speak three languages.
4. _____ college students major in languages.
   _____ the colleges here teach several different languages.
5. _____ students take two foreign languages in high school.
   In my class, _____ us studied two foreign languages.

In conversation

People usually say *everybody* and *nobody*, not *all people* or *no people*.

✗ Common errors

Remember to use *a* in *a lot of*.

A lot of students study English. (NOT ~~Lot of~~ students study English.)

3 Building vocabulary

A 🔊 **2.18** Listen and say the subjects. Circle your three favorite subjects. Tell a partner.

| algebra | economics | band | orchestra | choir | geometry | drama | physics | gymnastics | art |
| history | geography | track | chemistry | dance | calculus | biology | literature | computer studies |

Word sort Put the subjects above into the categories below. Can you think of other subjects?

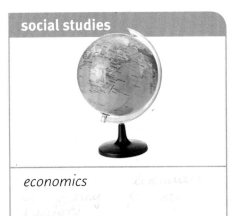
social studies

economics

music

choir

science

biology

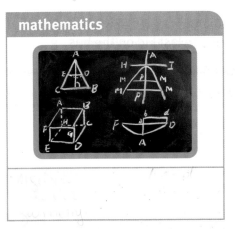
mathematics

physical education (P.E.)

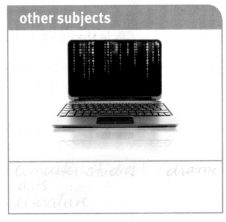
other subjects

Computer studies   drama
arts
literature

About you **Pair work** Talk about each subject above. Use the expressions below or use your own ideas. What do you have in common?

📙 Vocabulary notebook p. 52

I took / didn't take . . .   I was good / bad at . . .   I was / wasn't interested in . . .   I liked / didn't like . . .

4 Survey What was your best subject?

About you **Class activity** Choose a subject and write it in the first question. Then ask your classmates the questions about high school (or last year). Keep a tally (卌) of the answers.

	Yes	No			Yes	No
1. Did you take _____ ?	☐	☐	4. Were your classes hard?	☐	☐
2. Was it your favorite subject?	☐	☐	5. Did you enjoy them?	☐	☐
3. Did you get good grades in it?	☐	☐	6. Did you hate them?	☐	☐

B Tell the class your results. What interesting information did you learn?

"Most of us took chemistry. But only a few of us were good at it. . . ."

(((Sounds right p. 138

1 Reading

A Brainstorm the word *teenager*. What do you think of? Make a class list.

teenager: parties, loud music, fights with parents

B Read the interview. What, if anything, do you have in common with Joe?

 Reading tip

After you read, reflect. Compare your answers to the questions with the interviewee's.

Teenage Years

AN INTERVIEW WITH JOE HODGSON. JOE GRADUATED FROM THE UNIVERSITY OF MANCHESTER, ENGLAND WITH A DEGREE IN GENETICS.

1. Where were you born? Did you spend your teens there?
I was born in a small town near Manchester. I spent my teens there until I went to university* when I was 18.

2. What's one thing you remember about school?
I had a lot of fun with all my friends, playing soccer and pool. We used to try and sneak out of school during breaks to go to the sweet shop* around the corner.

3. What were your best subjects in school and your worst?
My best subject was science, especially biology, and that's what I ended up doing for my degree. My worst subject was algebra. I was never very good at it.

4. How did you spend your free time?
I spent a lot of time playing sports – soccer, cricket, and handball. I also did a lot of music – I played trumpet in the school orchestra. I sang in the choir as well.

5. What fashions and trends do you remember from your teen years?
The fashion I remember most was "emo" fashion because that was something I used to wear. We wore slim-fit jeans, black T-shirts and like most of my friends, I had long hair.

6. What was the most difficult thing about being a teenager?
Being stuck between being a kid and being an adult – so trying to balance the two. I think most teens feel that way.

I wanted to be treated like a true adult some of the time, and like a kid at other times. It was frustrating when someone got the "wrong" age.

7. What's the happiest memory you have from your teen years?
I played handball for my college team, and my happiest memory was when I was picked to play for England when I was 17. It was such a great feeling when I heard the national anthem and knew I was representing my country.

8. Who or what influenced you when you were a teenager? What did you learn?
My parents influenced me a lot, although I only really appreciated it when I was older. Some of my best friends influenced me, too. They all taught me the value of hard work, and of being yourself and enjoying that.

9. What do you miss about your teen years?
I miss the lack of responsibility! Now I have to worry about so much stuff like work and money, so I miss being a teenager because everything was a lot easier then.

10. What's one piece of advice you would give to today's teenagers?
Enjoy it! Have lots of fun. It's a great time – so have a great time.

*go to university = go to college
*sweet shop = candy store

C Are these sentences true or false? Check (✓) *True* (T) or *False* (F). Can you correct the false ones?

		T	F
1.	Joe was born in Manchester.	☐	☐
2.	He liked to sneak out of school to go to the movie theater.	☐	☐
3.	His worst subject in school was biology.	☐	☐
4.	He wore black T-shirts and had long hair when he was in school.	☐	☐
5.	Joe's best memory was playing soccer for England when he was 17.	☐	☐
6.	Joe enjoyed having no responsibility as a teenager.	☐	☐

About you   **Pair work** Ask and answer three questions from the interview.

2 Listening A long time ago

🔊 **2.21** Listen to Colin talk about being a teenager in England many years ago. Complete the sentences by circling *a*, *b*, or *c*.

1.	Colin was a teenager	a. in the '40s.	b. in the '50s.	c. in the '60s.
2.	He quit school when he was	a. 13.	b. 14.	c. 15.
3.	His first job was	a. in a factory.	b. in a store.	c. on a farm.
4.	His main interest was	a. music.	b. buying clothes.	c. watching TV.
5.	His main regret is that he	a. spent a lot of money.	b. didn't take classes.	c. didn't have fun.

3 Writing An interview

A Write five interview questions to ask a classmate about when he or she was younger. Leave spaces for the answers.

1. Did you get along with your parents?

2. Were you a good student?

About you   **Pair work** Exchange your questions with a classmate. Write answers to your classmate's questions. Use the example and the Help note below to help you.

1. Did you get along with your parents?
Yes, most of the time. I got good grades, so that was no problem. We agreed on most things except for the car. We had a lot of fights about that.

Help note

Linking ideas: *except (for), apart from*

*We agreed on most things **except for** the car. We didn't agree on much **apart from** my best friend. They liked her.*

About you   **Pair work** Read your partner's answers. Ask questions to find out more information.

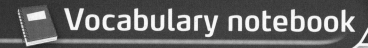
Learning tip *Grouping vocabulary*

You can group new vocabulary in different ways to help you remember it. For example, group things you can or can't do or things you are interested in or not interested in.

In conversation

Talk about school

The top four school subjects people talk about are:

1. math   3. physics
2. science   4. history

People say *math* almost ten times more than *mathematics*.

Complete the chart with the school subjects in the box. Add more ideas.

| art | chemistry | geography | math | P.E. |
| biology | English | history | music | physics |

I'm / I was good at . . .	I'm not / wasn't very good at . . .	I can't / couldn't do . . . at all.
Algebra		
Calculus		

I like / liked . . .	I hate / hated . . .	I'm not / wasn't very interested in . . .
Mathematics	geography	
	chemistry	

On your own

Walk around a large bookstore and look at the different sections. How many subjects do you know in English?

Travel?

✓ Can Do! Now I can . . .

✓ I can . . .   ? I need to review how to . . .

☐ talk about my family background and memories of growing up.

☐ discuss school subjects.

☐ say how many people do things.

☐ use *Well*, *Actually*, *No*, *wait*, and *I mean* to correct myself.

☐ understand conversations about childhood memories.

☐ understand someone talk about his teenage years.

☐ read an interview about being a teenager.

☐ write answers to interview questions.

Around town

☑ **Can Do!** In this unit, you learn how to . . .

Lesson A
- Ask about neighborhood places with *Is there . . . ?* and *Are there . . . ?*
- Say where places are with expressions like *next to*, *between*, etc.

Lesson B
- Ask for and give directions
- Offer and ask for help with *Can* and *Could*

Lesson C
- Check information by repeating words or using expressions like *Excuse me?*
- Ask "echo" questions like *It's where?* to check information

Lesson D
- Read an online guide to Istanbul
- Write a walking-tour guide

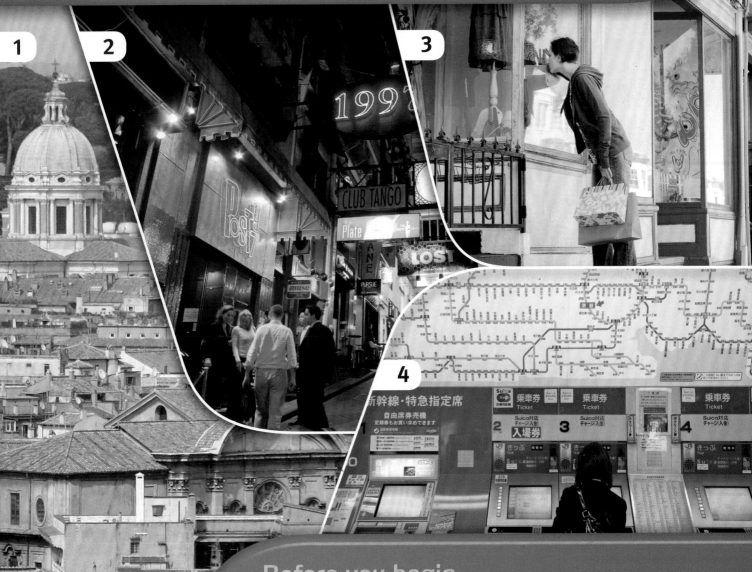

Before you begin . . .

Match each comment with a picture.

1 "There's a lot to see."

3 "It's great for shopping."

4 "It's easy to get around."

2 "There's a lot of nightlife."

What else can you say about each place?

53

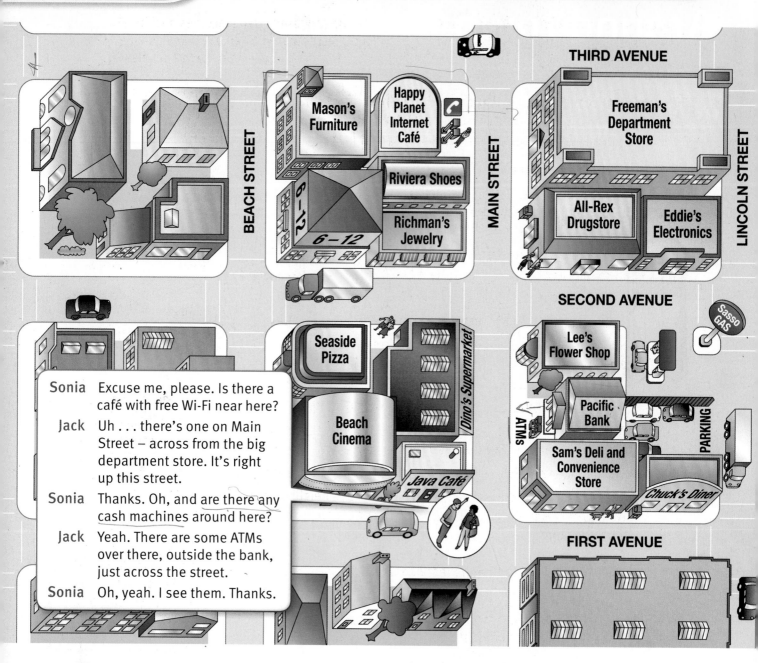

Sonia   Excuse me, please. Is there a café with free Wi-Fi near here?

Jack   Uh . . . there's one on Main Street – across from the big department store. It's right up this street.

Sonia   Thanks. Oh, and are there any cash machines around here?

Jack   Yeah. There are some ATMs over there, outside the bank, just across the street.

Sonia   Oh, yeah. I see them. Thanks.

1 Getting started

A Look at the map. What can you do at each place you see? Tell the class.

"Well, there's a furniture store. I guess you can buy tables and . . ."

B 🔊 2.22 Listen. Sonia is asking Jack for help. What is she looking for? Practice the conversation.

Figure it out   Can you complete these questions and answers? Practice with a partner.

1. A _____ a furniture store near here?

   B Yes, there's _____ on Beach Street.

2. A _____ any ATMs around here?

   B Yes, there are _____ cash machines just across the street.

2 Grammar *Is there? Are there?*; location expressions 🔊 2.23

Extra practice p. 145

Is there a café with free Wi-Fi near here?
Yes, **there is**. There's **one** on Main Street.
No, **there isn't**. There isn't **one** in this neighborhood.

Are there any cash machines near here?
Yes, **there are**. There are **some** outside the bank.
No, **there aren't**. There aren't **any** nearby.

A Look at the map on page 54. Complete the questions with *Is there a* or *Are there any*. Complete the answers with *one*, *some*, *any*, and location expressions. Then practice.

Driver ___Is there a___ bank around here?

Matt Yeah, there's ___one___ right ___on___ Main Street. It's ___next to___ the deli. Do you see Sam's Deli – just ___across___ the street?

Driver Oh, yeah. Can I park there? I mean, ___Is there a___ parking lot?

Matt Well, there's ___one___ just ___behind___ the bank, but the entrance is ___on___ Lincoln.

Driver ___Are there any___ public restrooms near there?

Matt No, there aren't ___any___ there, but there's a department store ___on the corner of___ Main and Third. I'm sure there are ___some___ there, ___inside___ the store.

Driver Thanks. Oh, and ___are there any___ shoe stores near here?

Matt Well, there's ___one___ on Main, ___between___ Second and Third Avenues. But that's about it.

Driver Okay. And one more thing – ___Is there a___ post office around here?

Matt Um . . . actually, there isn't ___one___ in this neighborhood. There's only a mailbox ___outside___ the drugstore – ___across from___ the shoe store.

Location expressions

behind   in front of

next to   between

inside   outside

on First Street   on the corner of Main and First

across (the street) from; opposite

B **Pair work** Now ask and answer questions about these places on the map.

- a jewelry store
- a gas station
- restaurants
- electronics stores
- a convenience store

✗ Common errors

Don't use *Is there* with plural nouns.

Are there any ATMs? (NOT ~~Is there~~ any ATMs?)

3 Speaking naturally Word stress in compound nouns

bookstore   *restroom*   *drugstore*

A 🔊 2.24 Listen and repeat the compound nouns above. Notice the stress pattern.

About you 🔊 2.25 Listen and complete the questions. Then ask and answer the questions with a partner.

1. Are there any nice _____ near your home?
2. Is there a _____ around here?
3. Is there a _____ in this area?
4. Are there any good _____ in this neighborhood?
5. Is there a good _____ near your home?
6. Are there any _____ around here?

55

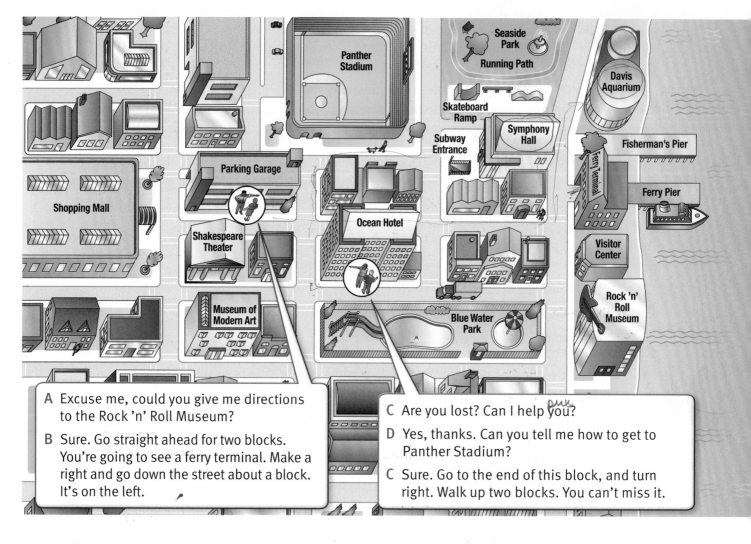

A Excuse me, could you give me directions to the Rock 'n' Roll Museum?

B Sure. Go straight ahead for two blocks. You're going to see a ferry terminal. Make a right and go down the street about a block. It's on the left.

C Are you lost? Can I help you?

D Yes, thanks. Can you tell me how to get to Panther Stadium?

C Sure. Go to the end of this block, and turn right. Walk up two blocks. You can't miss it.

1 Building vocabulary and grammar

A 🔊 2.26 **Listen to the conversations above, and follow the directions on the map. Then underline all the expressions for directions. Practice with a partner.**

Figure it out

Look at the information below. Find your location and destination on the map. Then complete the questions and put the directions in order.

1. **You're in the Ocean Hotel. Someone asks:**

   A Are you lost? ___Can___ I help you?

   B Thanks. _____ you give me directions to Symphony Hall?

   A [3] Um, then make a right.

   [2] Turn left again at the corner, and walk up two blocks.

   [4] It's right there, on the right.

   [1] Um, yes. When you go out of the hotel, turn left.

2. **You're outside the parking garage. You ask:**

   A ___Can___ you tell me how to get to the aquarium?

   B [5] The aquarium is going to be on your right.

   [2] You're going to see a ferry terminal.

   [1] Sure. Go straight ahead for two blocks.

   [3] Make a left.

   [4] Walk up the street about one block.

Vocabulary notebook p. 62

56

2 Grammar Offers and requests with *Can* and *Could* 2.27

Extra practice p. 145

Offers	Requests
Can I help you?	**Can** you help me?
What **can** I do?	**Can** you tell me how to get to the aquarium?
How **can** I help?	**Could** you give me directions?

In conversation

Can you . . . ? is more common than *Could you . . . ?* for requests.

People use *Could you . . . ?* to make their requests more polite.

Can you . . . ?

Could you . . . ?

A Look at the map on page 56. Some people are asking for directions at the Visitor Center. Complete the questions and directions.

1. A ________ you give me directions to the Museum of Modern Art? Is it far from here?
   B Uh, no, it's not far. So, go out of the door and turn ____________________ .
2. A ________ you recommend a place to go running?
   B Let me think. There's a running path in Seaside Park. Go ____________________ .
3. A Good morning. ________ I help you?
   B Yeah, thanks. ________ you tell me how to get to Panther Stadium?
   A Sure, you need to go ____________________ .
4. A I'm staying at the Ocean Hotel. ________ you give me directions from there to the aquarium?
   B Oh, no problem. Go ____________________ .
5. A Hello. ________ I help you? Oh, I'm sorry. You're waiting for a subway map. Here you go. So, the subway is just a short walk from here. Go ____________________ .
   B Thanks. Have a good day.

B Pair work Take turns asking for and giving directions to different places on the map on page 56.

3 Listening and speaking Finding your way around

A 2.28 **Look at the map on page 56 again. Listen to the concierge at the Ocean Hotel give directions to people. Where do they want to go? Write the places.**

1. ________ 2. ________ 3. ________ 4. ________

About you

Pair work Take turns asking the questions below and giving directions for the neighborhood you are in.

- Is there a place to go skateboarding near here?
- Could you recommend a cheap restaurant around here?
- Are there any cash machines within walking distance?
- Can you tell me how to get to the subway or to a bus stop?
- Could you give me directions to the nearest drugstore?
- Can you recommend a good place to go shopping?

Sounds right p. 138

A Is there a place to go skateboarding near here?
B Well, let me think. There's a skateboarding park behind the library. You just walk . . .

1 Conversation strategy Checking information

A What kind of information do people ask a concierge when they are staying in a hotel?
Make a class list.

They ask for directions to restaurants.

B 🔊 2.29 Listen. What places does the concierge recommend? Where does Maria decide to eat?

Concierge	Hello. Can I help you?
Maria	Um, are there any nice places to eat around here?
Concierge	Excuse me? Did you say places to eat?
Maria	Yes, but not fast food.
Concierge	OK. Well, there's a Mexican restaurant within walking distance.
Maria	Within walking distance?
Concierge	Yes. It's right down the street. It gets great reviews. Or there's a Vietnamese place on Park Avenue. That's really good.
Maria	I'm sorry? There's a Vietnamese place where?
Concierge	Park Avenue. But it's always busy. There's usually about a 15-minute wait.
Maria	Did you say fifteen or fifty?
Concierge	Fifteen.
Maria	Oh, OK. Well, that sounds good. Could you give me directions?

C **Notice** how Maria and the concierge check information. They repeat words as a question or use "checking" expressions. Find examples in the conversation.

> *"There's about a 15-minute wait."*
> *"Fifteen or fifty?"*

Checking expressions:
I'm sorry?
Excuse me?
Did you say . . . ?
What did you say?

D 🔊 2.30 Complete the conversations with the missing words. Then listen and check.
Practice with a partner and continue the conversations.

1. A Could you give me directions to the bus station?   B I'm sorry? Did you say the _____ ?
2. A Is there an Indonesian restaurant near here?   B Did you say Indian or _____ ?
3. A Do you have a number for a cab company?   B Excuse me? Did you say a _____ ?
4. A How do you get to the airport from here?   B Sorry, what did you say? The _____ ?
5. A Are there any good movies on this week?   B Any _____ , did you say?

2 Strategy plus "Echo" questions

In an "echo" question, you repeat something you heard, and you add a question word to check information you didn't hear.

There's a Vietnamese place on Park Avenue.

I'm sorry? There's a Vietnamese place where?

Here are some more examples:

A Is there a drugstore around here?

B I'm sorry, a what?

A It opens at 10:00.

B Excuse me? It opens at what time?

🔊 **2.31 Complete the conversations with "echo" questions. Use the words in the box. Then listen and check. Practice with a partner.**

how far	how much	✓what	what kind of	when	where

1. A So, are there any theme parks here?
    B I'm sorry, any _____*what*_____ ?

2. A Is there an outdoor swimming pool around here?
    B Actually, there is. It's opposite the park.
    A Excuse me? It's _____ ?

3. A You know, movie tickets cost $12. They're expensive.
    B They cost _____ ?

4. A They have great outdoor concerts every night until 10:00.
    B I'm sorry, until _____ ?

5. A So, are there any museums in the city?
    B Yeah. There's a science museum about 15 minutes away.
    A I'm sorry, it's _____ ?

6. A There are some good Thai restaurants here.
    B There are some good _____ restaurants?

In conversation

When people ask others to repeat information, they say *I'm sorry?* more often than *Excuse me?*

▬▬▬▬▬ *I'm sorry?*

▬▬ *Excuse me?*

3 Listening and strategies Tourist information

A 🔊 2.32 Listen to the start of six conversations at a visitor center. What do you think each person says next to check the information? Number the sentences 1 to 6.

☐ Excuse me? Fourteen or forty?   1 Did you say Thai?   ☐ I'm sorry? From where?

☐ I'm sorry. It's how far?   ☐ I'm sorry, a list of what?   ☐ Did you say roller skates?

B 🔊 2.33 Now listen to the complete conversations. How does the person working at the visitor center answer the questions above?

About you

Pair work Role-play conversations at a visitor center. Ask for information about places in your town or city, and check the information you hear.

A *Are there any good gift shops around here?*

B *Excuse me? What kind of shops?*

Free talk pp. 131 and 133

59

1 Reading

A What do you know about Istanbul? Make a class list.

It's in Turkey.

B Read the website below. Find one thing you didn't know about Istanbul and one thing you knew already.

Reading tip

Writers sometimes define words they use with a dash:
Enjoy a cup of chay – *Turkish tea.*

http://www.discoveringturkey...

3 days in Istanbul...

Is there any other city quite like Istanbul? Europe and Asia meet in this fascinating and lively place. With amazing sights, sounds, and smells on every corner, it's a must-see for everyone!

Day 1: **START WITH A WALKING TOUR** Your tour begins at Gülhane Park. Enjoy the shaded lawns and beautiful gardens, and walk toward the famous Topkapi Palace. The museum has incredible jewels, gold, and works of art. Then walk through the palace grounds for fabulous views across the Bosphorus. Walk back into the park and enjoy a cup of *chay* – Turkish tea – at one of the little outdoor cafés.

Outside the park, walk down one of the little cobblestone streets with traditional wooden houses. Find your way to the seventeenth century Blue Mosque – named for the blue tiles on its inside walls. Then walk north for a couple of blocks and visit the beautiful Hagia Sophia mosque – now a museum.

Day 2: **SHOP TILL YOU DROP** Start your day at the colorful and bustling Grand Bazaar. There are thousands of shops with everything from gold and silver to beautiful Turkish rugs. You'll find plenty of souvenirs here to take home with you. Then head north and continue to the fabulous spice market.

For a quick lunch, go to one of Istanbul's pastry shops and try a *borek* – a pastry with a cheese or meat filling. Delicious!

Spend the rest of your day exploring the fashionable area of Nisantasi, with its designer shops and exciting nightlife. Ready to drop? End your day at one of Istanbul's famous Turkish baths.

Day 3: **TAKE A TRIP ON THE RIVER** Today, take the local ferry from Eminonu to Anadolu Kavagi. Don't forget your camera so you can take spectacular photos of palaces, old houses, and forts along the way. Then, before the boat returns, be sure to have a leisurely lunch at one of the seafood restaurants. Or, if you're feeling energetic, hike up the hill for a fantastic view.

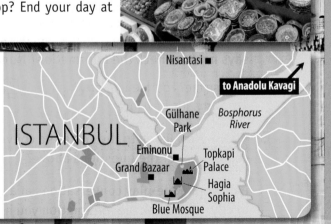

Nisantasi

to Anadolu Kavagi

ISTANBUL

Gülhane Park

Bosphorus River

Eminonu

Grand Bazaar

Topkapi Palace

Hagia Sophia

Blue Mosque

C Read the website again and answer the questions. Then compare with a partner.

1. Where can you do these things, according to the website?

   a. buy a Turkish rug

   b. walk around beautiful gardens

   c. see jewels and works of art

   d. drink Turkish tea

2. What is a *borek*?

3. What sights can you see on the boat trip?

4. How did the Blue Mosque get its name?

5. Which three places would you like to see on this tour? Why?

6. Are there any places you would *not* go to? Why?

2 Talk about it What are some of your favorite places?

Group work Discuss places in your town or city. Can you agree on the best place to do these things?

Is there . . .

▶ a good place to sit and watch people go by?

▶ a fun place to spend a rainy afternoon?

▶ a cheap (but good) place to eat?

▶ a quiet area to go for a walk or a jog?

▶ a good place to shop for electronics?

▶ an interesting museum?

▶ a neighborhood with a lot of cultural events?

▶ a neighborhood with lots of interesting nightlife?

3 Writing A walking-tour guide

A Read the guide to Rockville and the Help note below. Underline the expressions for giving directions.

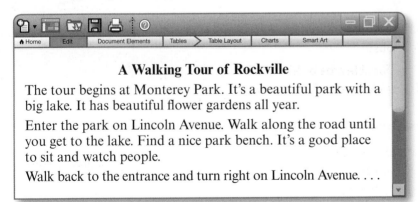

A Walking Tour of Rockville

The tour begins at Monterey Park. It's a beautiful park with a big lake. It has beautiful flower gardens all year.

Enter the park on Lincoln Avenue. Walk along the road until you get to the lake. Find a nice park bench. It's a good place to sit and watch people.

Walk back to the entrance and turn right on Lincoln Avenue. . . .

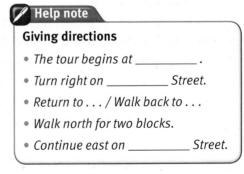

Help note

Giving directions

* *The tour begins at _____ .*
* *Turn right on _____ Street.*
* *Return to . . . / Walk back to . . .*
* *Walk north for two blocks.*
* *Continue east on _____ Street.*

About you Now write a guide for a walking tour in your city or town. Write about three different places and explain why they are worth visiting. Give directions to each place.

C **Group work** Read your classmates' guides. Then tell the group which tour you would like to take and why.

Learning tip *Drawing maps*

Draw and label a map to help you remember directions.

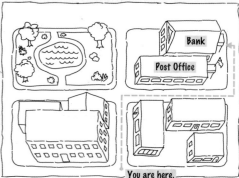

1 Use the map to number the directions to the bank below.

☐ Walk one more block.
☐ Turn right.
☐ 1 Walk up one block.
☐ Make a left.
☐ It's on the left, just past the post office.

2 Now draw your own map. Show the way from your home or class to a place you often go. Then write the directions to go with the map.

On your own

Buy or download a map of your town or city. Highlight the route from one place you know to another. Then write directions. Learn the directions.

Can Do! Now I can . . .

✓ I can . . .   ? I need to review how to . . .

☐ ask questions about places in a neighborhood.

☐ say where places are in a neighborhood.

☐ make offers like *Can I help you?*

☐ make requests like *Can you help me?*

☐ ask for and give directions.

☐ use expressions like *Excuse me?* to check information.

☐ ask "echo" questions to check information.

☐ understand directions and follow along on a map.

☐ understand conversations at a visitor center.

☐ read an online city guide.

☐ write a walking-tour guide for a neighborhood.

1 Unscramble the questions.

Put the words in the correct order to make questions. Then ask and answer the questions with a partner.

1. doing / are / next weekend / what / you ?
   What are you doing next weekend?

2. after class / going to / you / go shopping / are ?
   Are you going to go shopping after class?

3. it / rain / tomorrow / going to / is ?
   Is it going to rain tomorrow?

4. you / here / did / another city / from / move ?
   Did you move here from another city?

5. last year / you / did / on vacation / go / where ?
   Where did you go on vacation last year?

6. what / your / in school / favorite / was / subject ?
   What was your favorite subject in school?

7. are / a lot of / in / fun places / neighborhood / there / your ?
   Are there a lot of fun places in your neighborhood?

2 Can you complete this conversation?

Complete the conversation. Use the words and expressions in the box. Use capital letters where necessary. Then practice with a partner.

actually	✓are there any	him	I'm not sure	on	some	was born	where
and everything	did you say	I mean	my grandfather	one	until	what time	

A   *Are there any* nice gift stores around here?

B   *Did you say* gift stores? Um, there's *one* just across the street.
    Oh, *actually* no, it closed. But there are *some* in the mall.

A   Oh yeah. I need to get *my grandfather* something. It's his birthday next week.

B   Oh, really? How old is he going to be?

A   Well, he *was born* in 1948, so how old is that?

B   Oh, I'm not good at math. So, what are you going to get *him* ?

A   Um, *I'm not sure* .

B   Does he have any hobbies?

A   Well, he's pretty active. He's really into exercise.

B   Well, here's an idea. Take him to a bowling alley for his birthday.

A   Take him *where* ?

B   To a bowling alley. There's one *on* Fifth, *I mean* ,
    Sixth Avenue. And you can play pool and table tennis *and everything*
    It doesn't close *until* midnight.

A   It closes at *what time* ? Actually, that's a great idea. Thanks.

63

3 What can you remember?

A Add four words to each category, and compare with a partner. Ask questions to find out more information.

Events you are going to celebrate this year	Important dates for you	Places in town you go to often	Subjects you'd like to know more about
New Year's Eve	May 1st – my birthday	the bank	biology

A *How are you going to celebrate New Year's Eve?*
B *We're going out for dinner. How about you? Are you going to have a party, or . . . ?*

B Choose a category and survey your class or group. Report your findings to the class.

"Most of us are going to celebrate New Year's Eve."   *"Nobody is going to have a birthday party."*

4 Get it right!

A Can you complete these questions? Use the words in the box.

1. What's your city, I mean, your _____ like?
2. Are you going to any birthday parties, I mean, _____ this year?
3. Can you give me directions to a bank around here? I mean, a _____ ?
4. When did you learn to walk? I mean, when did you learn to _____ ?
5. What was your worst, I mean, _____ subject in school?

swim
best
neighborhood
weddings
post office

B Pair work Take turns asking the questions above. Use "vague" expressions in your answers. Check your partner's answers with "echo" questions.

A *What's your city, I mean, your neighborhood like?*
B *Well, I like it. There's a lot to do. We have a lot of cafés and restaurants and everything.*
A *I'm sorry. A lot of what?*

5 Do you know your city?

Pair work Write directions from your class to three places nearby. Then trade papers. Can your partner guess the places?

1. Cross the street, turn left, and walk up three blocks. This place is on the right, next to the bank. What is it?

1. A convenience store

UNIT 1 Find out about me!

1 Think of an interesting question you'd like to ask someone to get to know them better. Write your question on a small piece of paper, fold it, and put it in a pile.

Which do you prefer – hot weather or cold weather?

2 Class activity Take a piece of paper from the pile. Ask your classmates the question on your piece of paper. Find out one more piece of information from each classmate.

A *So, which do you prefer – hot weather or cold weather?*

B *Actually, I like cold weather. I like snow.*

A *Oh, I do too. So, do you ski?*

UNIT 2 Common interests

1 Complete the sentences below about your interests.

1. I enjoy _watching baseball._
2. I'm good at _____
3. I can't _____
4. I'm interested in _____
5. I would like _____
6. I like _____
7. I can _____
8. I think everybody _____

2 Group work Change the statements you made into questions to ask your group. Who is the same as you?

Questions	Names
1. Do you enjoy watching baseball?	Ichiro

A *Do you enjoy watching baseball?*

B *No, not really. I don't really understand the rules.*

C *Really? I love it. Baseball is my favorite sport.*

Free talk

Pair work Student B: Read about the apartment below. Student A: Read about the apartment on page 131. Take turns asking questions about the two apartments. Which one would you like to rent?

B *Are there any stores nearby?*

A *I'm sorry, are there any what? Stores? Let's see . . . um . . . well, there are . . .*

http://www.findyournewhome...

Apartment for rent – 1525 12th Avenue

Apartment features
2 bedrooms, 1 bathroom, living room with small kitchen
11th floor, elevator in building

Amenities
Laundromat on the corner of 12th Avenue and 15th Street
Pet-care service in building
24-hour security
Party room
Rooftop pool

Neighborhood
Convenient location. Within walking distance to a large shopping mall. Many restaurants and shops nearby. Convenience store across the street from the building. 5-minute walk to the nearest subway station.

UNIT **1** ◀))) **4.31** Listen and repeat the pairs of words. Notice the underlined sounds. Are the underlined sounds the same (S) or different (D)? Write *S* or *D*.

1. f<u>a</u>n / a<u>ff</u>ord ___S___

2. stra<u>ng</u>er / ma<u>j</u>or _____

3. o<u>f</u> / ha<u>v</u>e _____

4. deli<u>ci</u>ous / <u>sh</u>irt _____

5. do<u>g</u> / aller<u>g</u>ic _____

6. bro<u>k</u>e / <u>c</u>at _____

7. heal<u>th</u> / wea<u>th</u>er _____

8. li<u>s</u>ten / <u>s</u>alary _____

9. que<u>sti</u>on / quo<u>ta</u>tion _____

UNIT **2** ◀))) **4.32** Listen and repeat the words. Notice the underlined sounds. Are the sounds like the sounds in *j<u>oi</u>n*, *s<u>ou</u>nd*, *kn<u>ow</u>*, *p<u>u</u>zzle*, or *r<u>o</u>ck*? Write the words from the box in the correct columns below.

1. ab<u>ou</u>t	3. c<u>ou</u>ntry	5. f<u>o</u>lk	7. n<u>ow</u>	9. pr<u>o</u>gram
2. c<u>oi</u>n	4. enj<u>oy</u>	6. n<u>o</u>vel	8. p<u>o</u>p	10. s<u>o</u>mething

j<u>oi</u>n	s<u>ou</u>nd	kn<u>ow</u>	p<u>u</u>zzle	r<u>o</u>ck
	about			

UNIT **3** ◀))) **4.33** Listen and repeat the words. Notice the underlined sounds. Are the sounds like the sounds in *<u>o</u>ften*, *sn<u>ee</u>ze*, *f<u>oo</u>d*, or *st<u>ay</u>*? Write the words from the box in the correct columns below.

1. <u>a</u>wful	3. f<u>e</u>ver	5. head<u>a</u>che	7. m<u>ea</u>t
2. c<u>ou</u>gh	4. fl<u>u</u>	6. l<u>o</u>se	8. w<u>eigh</u>t

<u>o</u>ften	sn<u>ee</u>ze	f<u>oo</u>d	st<u>ay</u>
awful			

UNIT **4** ◀))) **4.34** Listen and repeat the words. Notice the underlined sounds. Which sound in each group is different? Circle the odd one out.

1. c<u>a</u>p   h<u>a</u>ppy   gr<u>a</u>duate   celebr<u>a</u>tion

2. y<u>ear</u>   w<u>ear</u>   c<u>are</u>ful   th<u>ere</u>

3. b<u>ir</u>thday   p<u>ar</u>ty   firew<u>or</u>ks   annive<u>r</u>sary

4. st<u>u</u>ff   Jan<u>ua</u>ry   m<u>u</u>sic   re<u>u</u>nion

Sounds right

🔊 **4.35** Listen and repeat the pairs of words. Notice the underlined sounds. Then circle the word with the same sound.

	Which word has the same sound?
1. geography and physics	pen or fan
2. biology and geometry	girl or joke
3. chemistry and orchestra	key or chair
4. actually and literature	chair or tie
5. grade and degree	job or gift

🔊 **4.36** Listen and repeat the words. Notice the underlined sounds. Are the sounds like the sounds in *across*, *cash*, *go*, or *shopping*? Write the words from the box in the correct columns below.

1. aquarium   3. block   5. electronics   7. over
2. bank   4. café   6. machine   8. video

across	cash	go	shopping
aquarium			

Extra practice

1 Lesson A Present of *be* and simple present (review)

A Complete the questions using the verbs given. Then write true answers.

1. ___*Are*___ (be) you a full-time student?
   Or _____ you _____ (have) a part-time job?

2. How many brothers and sisters _____ you _____ (have)?

3. What _____ (be) your mother's first name?

4. Where _____ your best friend _____ (live)? _____ he or she _____ (live) near you?

5. What _____ your best friend _____ (do)? _____ (be) he or she a full-time student?

6. What _____ (be) your neighbors like? _____ (be) they friendly?

7. How often _____ you _____ (get) English homework?
   How long _____ it _____ (take)?

8. _____ you and your friends _____ (go out) on Saturday nights?
   What _____ you _____ (do)?

9. How _____ your family _____ (spend) Sundays?
   _____ you _____ (get together) for lunch?

10. _____ your neighborhood _____ (have) a nice park?

About you **Pair work** Ask and answer the questions above. Ask follow-up questions to keep your conversation going.

> **✗ Common errors**
> Remember: simple present verbs with *he*, *she*, and *it* end in *-s*.
>
> *My brother works part time.*
> *He studies at night.*
> (NOT *My brother ~~work~~ part time. He ~~study~~ at night.*)

UNIT

1 Lesson B Responses with *too* and *either*

A Write responses with *too* or *either* to agree with these statements.

1. I sleep late on the weekends. _____I do, too_____
2. I don't live near a subway. _____I don't either_____
3. I'm an only child. _____I am not_____
4. I'm not a baseball fan. _____I'm not either_____
5. I have two brothers. _____I do_____
6. I can't stand soap operas. _____I can't either_____
7. I love reality shows. _____I do_____
8. I can stand on my head. _____I can't_____

About you **Pair work** Student A: Make the statements above true for you. Student B: Give your own responses. Then change roles. What do you have in common?

A I don't sleep late on the weekends.
B I don't either. I work on Saturdays.
A Me too. So that's one thing we have in common.

C Group work Find three things that you all have in common.

> **✗ Common errors**
> Don't use *too* to respond to negative statements.
>
> *A I don't have much money.*
> *B I don't either.*
> (NOT *I ~~don't too~~.*)

UNIT
2

Lesson A Verb forms

A Complete the sentences with the correct forms of the verbs given. Sometimes there is more than one correct answer.

1. A Do you like _____ (perform) on stage?
   B Yes. I enjoy _acting_ (act).
   C No, I don't. I hate _____ (do) anything like that in public.

2. A Are you interested in _____ (learn) to ski?
   B Oh, yeah. I'd like _____ (take) ski lessons.
   C No, not really. I prefer _____ (stay) indoors in the winter.

3. A Can you _____ (dance)?
   B Yes, I can. But I hate _____ (go) to discos and dance clubs.
   C No, I can't _____ (dance) at all. But I like _____ (watch) dance shows on TV.

4. A Do you enjoy _____ (go) to the movies?
   B Yes, I really like _____ (watch) movies on the big screen.
   C Yeah? I prefer _____ (watch) movies at home.

About
you Write your own responses to the questions above. Then ask and answer the questions with a partner.

UNIT
2

Lesson B Object pronouns; *everybody*, *nobody*

A Write object pronouns where they are necessary in the conversations. Then compare and practice with a partner.

1. A Do you like jazz?
   B Yeah, but I don't listen to ^it very much. Nobody in my family likes.

2. A I really love Miles Davis. He's my favorite trumpet player. Do you know?
   B Yeah. My whole family likes. He has so many albums.
   A Yeah, he does. They're all good, too. I like.

3. A I have two tickets for the Adele concert. She's my favorite singer. Do you want to go with?
   B Sure, I'd love to go. I love, too.

4. A I didn't know you play the banjo. I'd like to hear sometime.
   B Well, I have a band. We play in a coffee shop. Come and see on Friday.

> **Common errors**
>
> Use an object after *like*, *love*, etc.
>
> *Adele is my favorite singer. I like **her** very much.* (NOT *I like very much.*)

About
you **Group work** Make guesses about your group's interests and complete the sentences. Then read your sentences to the group. Are they true?

1. Everybody _____
2. Everyone _____
3. Nobody _____
4. No one _____

A I wrote, "Everybody in my group listens to jazz."   *B I don't like to listen to it, so that's not true.*

141

Lesson A Simple present and present continuous

A **Complete the things someone says about getting in shape. Use simple present or present continuous form of the verbs.**

1. My friend and I _are training_ (train) for a marathon.
   I normally __take__ (take) the bus to work, but these
   days I _____ (walk) all the way. And my friend
   _____ (spend) a lot of time at the gym these days.

2. I usually _____ (drink) a lot of soda, but right now,
   I _____ (drink) water instead.

3. This month, we _____ (get up) early, and I _____ (go)
   running. But generally we both _____ (sleep) late on the
   weekends.

4. My friend _____ usually _____ (not eat) breakfast, but
   now he _____ (have) eggs every morning.

5. I _____ (love) cheesecake, but this month I _____ (not eat) desserts. Our friends
   _____ (complain) because we _____ (not take) cookies to school right now.

> **✗ Common errors**
>
> Don't confuse the simple present
> and present continuous.
>
> *Normally I **walk** to school.*
> (NOT *Normally I'm walking to school.*)
>
> *I'm **eating** a special diet this week.*
> (NOT *I eat a special diet this week.*)

About you **Pair work** Are any of the sentences above true for you? What else are you doing differently
these days from what you usually do?

"Actually, I normally take the subway to school. But this week I'm walking some of the way."

Lesson B Joining clauses with *if* and *when*

About you **A** **Join the phrases with *when* or *if* to write true sentences about yourself.**

1. have a fever / take medicine
   When I have a fever, I usually take medicine.

2. lie down for a while / feel sick
   _____

3. get a stomachache / stay in bed
   _____

4. have a sore throat / drink hot tea with honey
   _____

5. go to the doctor / have a cough
   _____

6. take aspirin / have a headache
   _____

B **Pair work** What does your partner do in the situations above? Ask and answer questions.

   A *What do you do if you have a fever?*
   B *If I feel really hot, I put a cold towel on my head.*

UNIT **14** **Lesson A** Future with *be going to*; indirect objects

About you

Write questions (Q) with *be going to*. Then write your own answers (A), using indirect object pronouns where necessary.

1. what / you / give your mother for Mother's Day **Q** _____
   A _____

2. you / get your parents / something for their anniversary **Q** _____
   A _____

3. you / give your teacher / a thank-you card at the end of the year **Q** _____
   A _____

4. how / you / celebrate your birthday this year **Q** _____
   A _____

5. how old / your best friends / be on their next birthdays **Q** _____
   A _____

6. you / give someone a birthday present this month **Q** _____
   A _____

About you

Pair work Ask and answer the questions.

A What are you going to give your mother for Mother's Day?

B I'm probably going to buy her some flowers and get her a card.

UNIT **14** **Lesson B** Present continuous for the future; *be going to*

A Complete the conversations with the correct forms of the verbs. Use the present continuous when possible. Use *be going to* when you can't use the present continuous.

1. A _____ you _____ (go out) tonight?

   B Yeah, I _____ (take) my girlfriend to the Harbor Grill for dinner tonight for her birthday.
   I _____ (pick) her up in 30 minutes.

   A Wow. That place is fancy. It _____ (be) expensive.

   B Yeah, but she _____ (love) it.

2. A _____ you _____ (do) anything interesting tomorrow tonight?

   B Actually, yes. I _____ (meet) some friends at 8:00 to go to a concert.
   It _____ (be) so much fun.

3. A We _____ (play) softball tomorrow. Do you want to join us?

   B Sure. That sounds like fun. What time _____ you _____ (get together)?

   A We _____ (meet) at 11:00, but I heard it _____ (rain).

4. A Some of my classmates _____ (have) a party tomorrow night. Do you want to come?

   B Actually, I probably can't make it. I _____ (work) tomorrow from 5:00 to 10:00, and after that I think I _____ (be) too tired.

About you

Pair work Ask and answer the questions above. Give your own answers.

Illustration credits

Harry Briggs: 27, 79, 95, 100, 101, 134   **Bunky Hurter:** 10, 20, 30, 42, 52, 62 *(bottom)*, 74, 84, 94, 106, 116, 126   **Cambridge University Press:** 47 *(bottom left border)*, 55, 66 *(top right)*, 94 *(top)*   **Kim Johnson:** 25, 81, 91, 128, 132   **Scott Macneil:** 18, 54, 56, 60, 62 *(top)*, 145   **Frank Montagna:** 28, 124, 135, 136   **Q2A studio artists:** 69, 86, 111, 120   **Gavin Reece:** 31, 87, 103, 121   **Lucy Truman:** 4, 89, 96, 108, 127

Photography credits

Back cover: ©vovan/Shutterstock   **16, 17, 58, 59, 80, 90, 91, 102, 103, 122, 123** ©Cambridge University Press   **6, 7, 26, 27, 34, 38, 39, 44, 48, 49, 70, 71, 76, 112, 113** ©Frank Veronsky   **viii** *(left)* ©Rich Legg/Getty Images/RF; *(right)* ©Image Source/SuperStock   **1** *(clockwise from top left)* ©Corbis/SuperStock; ©Asia Images/ SuperStock; ©Jesse Wild/Total Guitar magazine/Getty Images; ©Thinkstock   **2** ©AsiaPix/SuperStock   **3** ©Thinkstock   **5** *(left to right)* ©Blue Jean Images/ SuperStock; *(tv)* ©Pakhnyushcha/Shutterstock; *(news)* ©Heather Wines/CBS via Getty Images; ©Flirt/SuperStock; ©GoodMood Photo/istockphoto   **7** *(bottom)* ©kristian sekulic/istockphoto   **8** *(left)* ©Steve Debenport/istockphoto; *(right)* ©Thinkstock   **9** ©Chris Pecoraro/istockphoto   **11** *(top row, left to right)* ©photovideostock/istockphoto; ©Nadya Lukic/istockphoto; ©YinYang/istockphoto *(bottom row, left to right)* ©Alberto Pomares/istockphoto; ©Ken Babione/ istockphoto; ©Thinkstock; *(tablet)* ©L_amica/Shutterstock   **12** ©Don Bayley/Getty Images/RF; *(background)* ©Feng Yu/Shutterstock   **14** *(top row, left to right)* ©Kevin Mazur/WireImage/Getty Images; ©Kevin Mazur/WireImage/Getty Images; ©George Pimentel/WireImage/Getty Images; ©Lucas Jackson/Reuters/Corbis *(bottom row, left to right)* ©Handout/WireImage/Getty Images; ©Roberta Parkin/Redferns via Getty Images; ©David Redfern/Redferns/Getty Images; ©TIZIANA FABI/ AFP/Getty Images   **15** ©Dougal Waters Photography Ltd/Getty Images/RF   **17** *(bottom, left to right)* ©Casey McNamara/Getty Images; ©Charlie Neuman/ZUMA Press/ Corbis; ©Exactostock/SuperStock; ©Thomas Trötscher/istockphoto   **18** *(top to bottom)* ©Tyler Olson/Shutterstock; ©nimu1956/istockphoto   **19** ©Ridofranz/ istockphoto   **21** *(clockwise from top left)* ©Alex Brosa/Getty Images; ©Design Pics/SuperStock; ©Chris Schmidt/Getty Images; ©Belinda Images/SuperStock; ©Nicolas McComber/istockphoto; ©Cultura Limited/SuperStock   **22** *(top row, left to right)* ©Jamie Carroll/istockphoto; ©Fotolia; ©Thinkstock *(bottom row, left to right)* ©digitalskillet/istockphoto; ©Thinkstock; ©Asia Images/SuperStock; *(background)* ©Natutik/Shutterstock   **23** ©Elena Ray/Shutterstock   **24** *(top row, left to right)* ©age fotostock/SuperStock; ©B BOISSONNET/BSIP/SuperStock; ©MAY/BSIP/SuperStock; ©laflor/istockphoto *(bottom row, left to right)* ©Blend Images/ SuperStock; ©Jens Koenig/Getty Images; ©flyfloor/Getty Images; ©Science Photo Library/SuperStock   **25** ©DEX IMAGE/Getty Images/RF   **29** *(top row, left to right)* ©Thinkstock; ©Thinkstock; ©age fotostock/SuperStock; ©Alexander Fortelny/istockphoto; *(middle, all photos)* ©Thinkstock; *(bottom, left to right)* ©Thinkstock; ©Silvia Jansen/istockphoto   **33** *(clockwise from top left)* ©Thinkstock; ©Image Source/Getty Images; ©SuperStock; ©Cultura Limited/SuperStock; ©Andres Rodriguez/SuperFusion/SuperStock   **35** ©age fotostock/SuperStock   **36** *(top row, left to right)* ©Thinkstock; ©Donna Coleman/istockphoto; ©Blue Jean Images/SuperStock *(bottom row, left to right)* ©bikeriderlondon/Shutterstock; ©Exactostock/SuperStock; ©Burke/Triolo Productions/Getty Images   **37** ©hanibaram/istockphoto   **39** *(bottom, left to right)* ©Charlie Neuman/ZUMA Press/Corbis; ©Christophe Boisvieux/Corbis   **40** *(left to right)* ©AP Photo/Larry Crowe; ©Benjamin Loo/istockphoto; ©Jupiterimages/Getty Images/RF; *(background)* ©Paprika/Shutterstock   **41** *(background)* ©Devor/Shutterstock   **42** *(notebook background)* ©Elena Schweitzer/Shutterstock   **43** *(clockwise from top left)* ©age fotostock/SuperStock; ©LEMOINE/BSIP/SuperStock; ©Blend Images/ SuperStock; ©Fancy Collection/SuperStock   **46** *(top row, left to right)* ©Nancy Louie/istockphoto; ©Fancy Collection/SuperStock; *(bottom row, left to right)* ©Juanmonino/istockphoto; ©Fancy Collection/SuperStock   **47** *(top row, left to right)* ©Picsfive/Shutterstock; © dafne/Shutterstock; ©Thinkstock *(bottom row, left to right)* ©hh5800/istockphoto; ©Christopher Futcher/istockphoto; ©Thinkstock   **49** *(bottom)* ©Cusp/SuperStock   **50** ©Ron Levine/Getty Images   **51** ©Thinkstock   **53** *(clockwise from top right)* ©Jupiterimages/Thinkstock; ©Exactostock/SuperStock; ©age fotostock/SuperStock; ©Henry Westheim Photography/Alamy   **57** ©Thinkstock   **59** *(bottom)* ©Ivan Solis/istockphoto   **60** *(top to bottom)* ©Thinkstock; ©Reimar Gaertner/age fotostock/SuperStock; *(background)* ©Thinkstock   **61** *(top to bottom)* ©GUIZIOU Franck/hemi/Hemis.fr/SuperStock; ©freesoulproduction/Shutterstock   **63** ©imagebroker.net/SuperStock   **65** *(clockwise from top left)* ©Glow Images - 40260.com/SuperStock; ©Thomas Sztanek/Purestock/SuperStock; ©Fancy Collection/SuperStock; ©Maskot/Getty Images   **66** ©Wendy Carter/ istockphoto   **67** ©Beyond/SuperStock   **68** *(bathing suit)* ©sagir/Shutterstock; *(sandals)* ©Shevel Artur/Shutterstock; *(towel)* ©Mike Flippo/Shutterstock; *(cooler)* ©Danny E Hooks/Shutterstock; *(hat)* ©windu/Shutterstock; *(mp3 player)* ©Thinkstock; *(sunglasses)* ©Uros Zunic/Shutterstock; *(insect repellent)* ©andrea crisante/ Shutterstock; *(tent)* ©trekandshoot/Shutterstock; *(GPS)* ©Thinkstock; *(camera)* ©Chiyacat/Shutterstock; *(scissors)* ©Phakkaphon Juawanich/Shutterstock; *(sleeping bag)* ©Mark Herreid/Shutterstock; *(first-aid kit)* ©Alan Crawford/istockphoto; *(pajamas)* ©Suljo/istockphoto; *(tablet computer)* ©Sashkin/Shutterstock; *(flashlight)* ©Artur Marfin/Shutterstock; *(batteries)* ©grekoff/Shutterstock; *(charger)* ©zirconicusso/Shutterstock; *(e-reader)* ©Ziva_K/istockphoto; *(brush)* ©FomaA/ Shutterstock; *(hair dryer)* ©Nordling/Shutterstock; *(makeup)* ©Sergiy Kuzmin/Shutterstock; *(shampoo)* ©Alex011973/Shutterstock; *(soap)* ©Robert Red/Shutterstock; *(razor)* ©Lusoimages/Shutterstock; *(toothpaste)* ©Kenneth C. Zirkel/istockphoto; *(toothbrush)* ©George Dolgikh/Shutterstock; *(sunscreen)* ©Africa Studio/ Shutterstock   **71** *(bottom)* ©Exactostock/SuperStock   **72** *(top to bottom)* ©Fotostudio Jaap Woets; ©EcoCamp Patagonia; ©The Safari Collection; *(tablet)* ©L_amica/ Shutterstock   **73** *(top row, left to right)* ©Hugh Rooney/Eye Ubiquitous/Corbis; ©Derek Croucher/Getty Images; ©imagebroker.net/SuperStock *(bottom)* ©Fotolia; *(background)* ©Nik Merkulov/Shutterstock   **75** *(clockwise from top left)* ©Lisa F. Young/istockphoto; ©Digital Vision/Thinkstock; ©Lucas Allen/Corbis; ©Sheltered Images/SuperStock   **77** ©peepo/istockphoto   **78** (clockwise from top left) ©Thinkstock; ©Thinkstock; ©Frank Short/Istockphoto; ©Elena Elisseeva/ Shutterstock   **82** ©Don Farrall/Getty Images   **83** *(top row, left to right)* ©Hans Laubel/istockphoto; *(news)* ©John Paul Filo/CBS vis Getty Images; ©George Doyle/ Thinkstock; ©Tatyana Nyshko/istockphoto; ©RelaXimages/SuperStock; *(bottom row, left to right)* ©moodboard/SuperStock; ©Stephen Chiang/Getty Images; ©Image Source/SuperStock; ©Artazum/Shutterstock   **84** *(left to right)* ©Ramsey Blacklock/istockphoto; ©ShutterWorx/istockphoto; ©Sawayasu Tsuji/istockphoto; ©Yenwen Lu/istockphoto   **85** *(clockwise from top right)* ©Paula Connelly/istockphoto; ©Exactostock/SuperStock; ©Exactostock/SuperStock; ©Tom England/ istockphoto   **86** *(top to bottom)* ©Thinkstock; ©Thinkstock; ©Maria Teijeiro/Thinkstock   **88** *(main photo)* ©Exactostock/SuperStock; *(top to bottom)* ©Kasiap/ Shutterstock; ©Thinkstock; ©Thinkstock; ©Levent Konuk/Shutterstock; ©wavebreakmedia/Shutterstock   **92** *(clockwise from top left)* ©Thinkstock; ©Thinkstock; ©Jupiterimages/Thinkstock; ©Stockbyte/Thinkstock   **97** *(clockwise from top left)* ©Hocus Focus Studio/istockphoto; ©Exactostock/SuperStock; ©Radius/ SuperStock; ©Blend Images/SuperStock; ©Exactostock/SuperStock; *(inset)* ©Shelly Perry/istockphoto   **98** *(top row, left to right)* ©Jon Feingersh/MediaBakery; ©SZE FEI WONG/istockphoto; ©laflor/istockphoto; *(bottom row, left to right)* ©George Doyle/Thinkstock; *(inset)* ©Exactostock/SuperStock; ©BananaStock/ Thinkstock   **104** *(tablet)* ©L_amica/Shutterstock   **107** ©Steve Debenport/istockphoto   **110** *(top row, left to right)* ©Goldmund Lukic/istockphoto; ©Michael Bodmann/istockphoto; ©laflor/istockphoto; ©Fancy Collection/SuperStock; *(middle row, left to right)* ©Junko Yokoyama/Getty Images; ©Sanjay Deva/istockphoto; ©James Woodson/Thinkstock; ©Amos Morgan/Thinkstock; *(bottom row, left to right)* ©Jamie Choy/istockphoto; ©wrangel/istockphoto; ©Exactostock/SuperStock; ©Fancy Collection/SuperStock   **112** *(bottom)* ©Jim Barber/Shutterstock   **113** *(bottom, left to right)* ©vipflash/Shutterstock; ©Leonard Adam/Getty Images; ©Venturelli/Getty Images for P&G Prestige; ©Henry S. Dziekan III/Getty Images; ©s_bukley/Shutterstock; ©Francois Durand/Getty Images   **114** *(top to bottom)* ©Thinkstock; ©selimaksan/istockphoto; ©Todd Smith istockphoto; ©AlexKol Photography/Shutterstock; ©coloroftime/istockphoto; ©sam100/Shutterstock; ©Radu Razvan/istockphoto   **117** *(clockwise from top right)* ©Westend61/SuperStock; ©Westend61/SuperStock; ©Fancy Collection/SuperStock; ©Ocean/ Corbis   **118** *(clockwise from top right)* ©Christopher Futcher/istockphoto; ©Thinkstock; ©Juergen Bosse/istockphoto; ©Thinkstock; ©YinYang/istockphoto   **123** *(bottom)* ©Yong Hian Lim/istockphoto   **124** *(background)* ©URRRA/Shutterstock   **129** *(left to right)* ©Belinda Images/SuperStock; ©Thinkstock; ©YinYang/ istockphoto   **130** ©Elena Kalistratova/istockphoto   **131** ©Aleksandrs Gorins/istockphoto   **133** ©Oleg Zabielin/Shutterstock   **134** *(top row, left to right)* ©ewg3D/ istockphoto; ©Henrik Jonsson/istockphoto; ©Linda Johnsonbaugh/istockphoto; ©zveiger alexandre/istockphoto; ©DrGrounds/istockphoto; ©Rich Legg/ istockphoto; *(bottom row, left to right)* ©Yulia Popkova/istockphoto; ©Jon Arnold/Jon Arnold Images/SuperStock; ©LEMOINE/BSIP/SuperStock; ©Stockbroker/ SuperStock   **150** ©michaeljung/Shutterstock

Text credits

While every effort has been made, it has not always been possible to identify the sources of all the materials used, or to trace the copyright holders. If any omissions are brought to our notice, we will be happy to include the appropriate acknowledgements on reprinting.

50 Interview used with permission of Joseph Hodgson.